**Words from John's readers:**

"John Pavlovitz's words soothe my soul and help me not feel so alone! He gives voice to thoughts and feelings that I felt no one shared until I came across his writings. He speaks the words I think and feel!" —Lisa Huesman

"I'm thankful for John's words because they help me feel that I'm not alone. His voice speaks for those of us in the 'Humane Middle' who so many times feel lost in the cruelty of this world. I hope he will keep saying things that need to be said. We need to hear them." —Trena B.

"John was a lifeline after the shock of the 2016 election. His grief was my grief; his rage, my rage. His was a companion in the desert. John was a clear, resonating voice of the Resistance when it was still just a whisper." —Lance Harshbarger

"John Pavlovitz tells it like it is—and as it should be. He cares more, advocates more, and nurtures more than any one person should be able to. Whether reading his social media posts or meditating on his reflections, I am uplifted and challenged to be a better human." —Carol Hawley

"We are always listening for John's clear and courageous voice rising above the noise of our times. He reminds us of what it truly means—and what it takes— to love one another." —Patricia and Ron Higgins

"John is a gifted writer; he has the ability to put into words what is in so many of our hearts. His blog has been a lifesaver in these troubling times. I highly recommend that you read all of his books." —Kellie Rorrer

"John's words express what I passionately feel in the core of my soul. Thank you for saying what I cannot articulate." —Danielle Marion-Doyle

"Not everyone has John's gift for saying stuff that needs to be said. Those who do help the rest of us find our voices." —Grant Grissom

"A calm voice of reason in a chaotic world. I look forward to every column."
—Linda W. Wahlig

"John puts words to my thoughts and comfort to my heart. He is tender, straight-forward, and sometimes blunt. Yet, in the end, his words tell a story that stays with me all day." —Carol Vandenbosch

"Not only does John have a way of knowing what needs to be said—he's also tapped into what many people are really feeling and thinking. He masterfully articulates my thoughts and observations, and I am constantly sharing his work with my friends and family." —Milissa Wilk Larstanna

"John is straightforward, relatable, and compassionate. He is hope."
—Karen Mates

"John is the light in a time of darkness." —Rachel W.

"I love that, as a liberal-minded Christian, there's a calm voice of reason infiltrating the nonsense of the past few years. Keep it up!" —Alicia Ruzycki

# Stuff That Needs To Be Said

JOHN PAVLOVITZ

**Published by:** Pavlovitz Design

**Cover and Text Design by:** Jennifer Pavlovitz

**ISBN:** 978-0-578-68250-1

*This book is dedicated to my past and current financial supporters, either through Patreon or elsewhere. Thank you for partnering with me in a tangible way, for being a source of community, and for providing a steady presence in so many turbulent seasons. While tens of millions have read these words, you have sacrificed so that they could be written. I'm grateful to you all for allowing me to say stuff that needs to be said.*

*Thanks to my amazing wife, Jennifer, for the superb cover design and layout of the book, and for always making me look better (in print and everywhere else). No one has done more to help me say what I feel I need to say.*

*Special thanks to Mary Lib Morgan for editing this collection and for being such a great light in the world.*

# Contents

## Part 2: Stuff That Needs To Be Said About America, Race, and Politics

**Part 3: Stuff That Needs To Be Said**
**About Life, Death, Grief, and Depression**     **187**

# Introduction

On March 18th, 2012, I published my first blog post. At that time, the blog was called *The Daily Dough*—a play on Jesus' teaching about praying for our "daily bread." I was the student pastor of one of the hundred largest United Methodist churches in America, and I began writing the blog to reach parents of teenagers in our massive community and other youth ministers around the country who needed encouragement and inspiration. The writing was trying to be bold and boundary-pushing, but was always decidedly, safely, and appropriately *Christian*. Looking back, I can see how careful my words were: the way I needed to couch everything in the appropriate religious language to make sure I wouldn't draw the ire of parents or raise alarms on the staff or be summoned to the principal's (lead pastor's) office. When speaking about sexuality, for example, I could say that we should *love* LGBTQ people (that was acceptable party line code language), but I couldn't say that I was fine with them staying the way they were—and I sure as heck couldn't say that I didn't believe being LGBTQ was a sin.

So, I did what so many pastors do when their convictions bump up against their livelihoods: I softened my language, I tried to say things without really saying them, and ultimately, I was less than fully authentic. As I walked further down the road of ministry and grew more entrenched in Church culture, I became more and more aware of the tension between the person I thought I was supposed to be as I followed Jesus—and the pastor I was *expected* to be. I began to see the hypocrisies and inequities organized religion was perpetuating (and that I was partially complicit in), and though I could refer vaguely to these things and even gently confront them—I could never say everything.

One December afternoon that year, though, everything changed. My wife called me while I was waiting in a food court line to ask if I'd heard about a shooting at an elementary school in a place called Sandy Hook. I remember feeling the ground cave in around me as she told me what had happened. By the time I got home and the unfathomable scale of the tragedy was coming into view, the heavy grief I felt turned to scalding anger when I saw what high-profile evangelists and Christian politicians were saying: the way they were framing this mass murder as some judgement by God against America for removing prayer from schools; how they were politicizing the pain of other people. My blood boiled and I ran to the computer, as it was the only way I felt I could push back against their cruelty and to defend grieving families. This time, I wasn't careful with my words and I didn't talk *around* how I felt—I just wrote clearly from the deepest recesses of my heart and then I hit *send*. I wasn't writing; I was bleeding. That post reached far outside the small community of readers I'd amassed, and I soon knew my writing was never going to be the same again. Neither was my pastoral ministry. In the blog and at my church, I felt a new responsibility to speak explicitly into matters of equality and diversity and justice, even if it caused me turbulence. (This would be a road to eventual ministry termination, and to an exponentially larger audience, but that's a story you can find in my book *A Bigger Table*.)

I soon retitled the blog *Stuff That Needs To Be Said*, not because I imagined everyone agreed these were words that actually *needed* to be said—in fact many would be quite certain they were not—but because *I* needed to say them. They were and are the burdens on my heart—the things that keep me up at night, the questions and the fears and the affirmations that will not be contained. If you're reading this, hopefully you've found something of yourself in the writing, some of your story reflected in mine, some affinity to what I've shared with the world. I hope they've inspired or challenged or changed you in some small way: that they've allowed you to question your assumptions, to name the injustice you see, and have given you permission to be the most authentic version of yourself, regardless of the cost. Most of all, I hope these words have left you feeling seen, heard, and known—and that they've moved you to say whatever stuff you feel needs to be said.

Thanks for reading and be greatly encouraged.

John

# PART ONE

# Stuff That Needs To Be Said About Religion, Faith, Sex, and the Church

# CHAPTER ONE

# If I Have LGBTQ Children

Sometimes I wonder if I'll have LGBTQ children.

I'm not sure if other parents think about this, but I often do.

Maybe it's because there are many people in my family and circle of friends who identify as gay, lesbian, bisexual, transgender, and questioning. It's in my genes and in my tribe.

Maybe it's because as a pastor of students, I've seen and heard the horror stories of LGBTQ Christian kids from both inside and outside the closet trying to be part of the Church.

Maybe it's because as a Christian, I interact with so many professed followers of Jesus who find "homosexuality" to be the greatest of sins, and who make that abundantly clear at every conceivable opportunity.

For whatever reason, it's something that I ponder frequently. As a pastor and a parent, I wanted to make some promises to you and to my two kids right now:

1) *If I have LGBTQ children, you'll all know it.*

Our kids won't be our family's best kept secret unless *they* choose to be. Whatever about their lives they wish to share will be shared with joy and without apology.

I won't talk around them in conversations with others. I won't speak in code or vague language; I won't try to pull the wool over anyone's eyes; and I won't try to spare the feelings of those who may be older or easily offended or uncomfortable. Childhood is difficult enough, and most LGBTQ kids spend their entire existence being horribly, excruciatingly uncomfortable because they need to be inauthentic. I'm not going to put my children through any more unnecessary discomfort just to make Thanksgiving dinner a little easier for a third cousin with misplaced anger issues.

If my children come out, we'll be out as a family.

2) *If I have LGBTQ children, I'll pray for them.*

I won't pray for them to be made "normal." I've lived long enough to know that if my children do come to identify as LGBTQ, that is their normal.

I won't pray that God will heal or change or fix them. I will pray for God to protect them from the ignorance and hatred and violence that the world will throw at them simply because of who they are. I'll pray that God shields them from those who will despise them and wish them harm; who will curse them to Hell and put them through hell without ever knowing them at all. I'll pray that they enjoy life; that they laugh and dream and feel and forgive—and that they love God and all people.

Above all, I'll pray that my children won't allow the horrible treatment they might receive from some of God's misguided followers to keep them from pursuing God.

3) *If I have LGBTQ children, I'll love them.*

I don't mean some token, distant, tolerant love that stays at a safe arm's length. It will be an extravagant, open-hearted, unapologetic, lavish, embarrassing-them-in-the-school-cafeteria, kissing-them-in-public kind of love.

I won't love them *despite* their sexuality and I won't love them *because* of it. I will love them for the same reasons I *already* do—simply because they're sweet and funny and caring and smart and kind and stubborn and flawed and original and beautiful... and *mine.*

If my kids are LGBTQ, they may doubt a million things about themselves and about this world, but they'll never doubt for a second whether or not their Daddy is over-the-moon crazy about them.

4) *If I have LGBTQ children...I have LGBTQ children.*

If my kids are going to be gay or bisexual or transgender or lesbian, well...they pretty much already are.

God has already created them and wired them and placed the seed of who they are within them. Psalm 139 says that God "stitched them together in their mother's womb." The incredibly

intricate, microscopic stuff that makes them uniquely *them*—
*once-in-History* souls? It's already been uploaded into their very
cells.

Because of that, there isn't a coming deadline on their identity
or orientation that their mother and I are working feverishly
toward. I don't believe there's some magical expiration date by
which time she and I need to somehow do or say or pray just the
right things to get them to "turn straight" or forever lose them
to *the other side*.

They are, today, simply a younger version of who they will be—
and today they're pretty darn great.

I fully realize that many of you may be offended by all of this.
I know my words here may be especially difficult if you are a
religious person with a particular theological stance. Perhaps
you find the whole topic unsettling.

As you've been reading, you may have been rolling your
eyes, clicking the roof of your mouth, or drafting familiar
Scriptures to send me. You may be praying for me to repent,
or preparing to unfriend me, or writing me off as a sinful, evil,
Hell-bound heretic; but let me say with as much gentleness and
understanding as I can muster—I really couldn't care less.

This isn't about you. This is a whole lot bigger than you.

You're not the one I waited on breathlessly for nine months.

You're not the one I wept with joy for when you were born.

You're not the one I bathed and fed and rocked to sleep through
a hundred intimate, midnight snuggle sessions.

You're not the one I taught to ride a bike, whose scraped knee I kissed, and whose tiny, trembling hand I held when you got stitches.

You're not the one whose head I love to smell and whose face lights up when I come home at night and whose laughter is like music to my weary soul when the world seems wrong.

You're not the one who gives my days meaning and purpose and whom I adore more than I ever thought I could adore anything or anyone.

And you're not the one I hope to be with when I take my last precious breaths on this planet, gratefully looking back on a lifetime of shared treasures and resting in the knowledge that I loved you well and was loved well by you.

If you're a parent, I don't know how you'll respond if you find out your children are LGBTQ, but I pray you consider it. I pray you prepare yourself.

Because one day, despite your perceptions of your kids or how you've parented or what signs you did or didn't see, you may need to respond in real-time to a frightened, frantic, hurting child—one whose sense of peace and identity and acceptance, whose heart and very life may be placed in your hands in a way you never imagined. You'll need to respond—and I don't want you to blow it.

If that day should ever come for me as a parent, if my children should ever come out to me—as much as I'm able, this is the Dad I hope I'll be to them.

# CHAPTER TWO

# The Church of Not Being Horrible

I'm tired.

I'm tired of professed Christians preaching about a Jesus whom they seem to have no interest at all in emulating; I'm tired of religious people being a loud, loveless noise in the world while supposedly claiming to speak for a God who *is* love.

I know the world is tired of such people.

I'm fairly certain that God is, too.

I'm starting a new church—the Church of Not Being Horrible.

Our mission statement is simply this: *Don't be horrible to people.*

Don't treat them as less worthy of love, respect, dignity, joy, and opportunity than you are.

Don't create caricatures of them based on their skin color, their religion, their sexual orientation, the amount of money they have, the circumstances they find themselves in.

Don't seek to take things away from them that you already enjoy in abundance: civil rights, clean water, education, marriage, access to healthcare.

Don't tell someone's story about why *they* are poor, depressed, addicted, victimized, alone. Let them tell their own story, and believe they know it better than you do.

Don't imagine that your experience of the world is everyone's experience of the world. Don't assume that the ease, comfort, support, and affection you have received are universal.

Don't be preoccupied with how someone experiences God, how they define family, whom they love. Cultivate your faith, family, and marriage alone.

The central question at any given moment in my new church is: *Am I being horrible right now?* If one concludes that they are, they endeavor not to do so. If they are unsure, they allow other people to help them see their horrible blind spots of privilege, prejudice, and ignorance—and then they respond.

In other words, our sacred calling is to be decent, to be kind, to be compassionate, to be whatever it is that we believe this place is lacking: to be the kind of people the world needs—and it definitely needs fewer horrible people *and less horrible people* these days.

The Church of Not Being Horrible will gather every week to celebrate the inherent goodness of people. We'll share stories of the ways we succeeded in being less horrible to our families, coworkers, and strangers, and we'll challenge ourselves to be even less horrible in the coming week. We'll do this faithfully, repeatedly, and passionately, and hopefully we'll begin to watch the world around us gradually become less angry, less bitter, less painful—less horrible.

I'm not sure such a religion will catch on, as being horrible seems to be trending these days among religious people, but I think it's worth a shot. I think it might alter the homes, marriages, and communities we're living in, if not the planet our feet are planted on. It might renovate our very hearts...hearts so prone to being horrible. It might help us become the best versions of ourselves that we are able to be.

If you're interested in joining the church, you don't need to pray a magic prayer. You don't have to attend a membership class or recite any creeds or take a test or promise to give financially. There are no theological or bureaucratic hoops to jump through.

There is no conversion, there is only commencement. You simply begin right where you are, at this very moment—seeking to be less horrible to the people you live with, work with, come across in the street, interact with online, see from a distance. That's it.

It may seem like a low bar to set, but it's actually a beautiful and somewhat novel aspiration for a church lately: making the world less cruel, less violent, less insulting—less horrible.

If you feel like that might be a religion worthy of your days... let's have some church, friends.

# CHAPTER THREE

# Christians Are Supposed to Care About People

I used to think I was a Christian.

I was raised in a Christian home and went to a Christian school. After a few meandering spiritual wilderness years, I attended a Christian seminary, became a Christian pastor, and have served in Christian churches for most of the past twenty-five years of my life.

I've read and studied and preached the Scriptures extensively; led community Bible studies and student retreats and overseas mission trips; ministered in tiny rural chapels and massive gleaming megachurches.

As a result of these decades immersed in the Christian tradition both personally and vocationally, I thought I had at least the gist of Jesus.

Now I think maybe I've been doing this wrong all these years.

For my entire life, I assumed something that perhaps I shouldn't have: I thought Christians were supposed to care about people— not necessarily agree with them or believe what they believe or even like them, but see them each as specific and unique image-bearers of the Divine, to want and to work for *Shalom* for them: wholeness, happiness, peace, safety, rest.

I grew up believing that one of the markers of a life that emulates Jesus was a heart capable of being broken at the distress of other human beings around you: when they are hungry and hurting; when they are homeless and afraid; when they grieve and feel alone; when they believe they are unloved and forgotten; when tragedy befalls them and when injustice assails them. These things are supposed to move the needle within us if Jesus is present.

And in all my years of criss-crossing the Gospels in both study and reflection, I never once found a Jesus who piled burdens on already burdened people or rejoiced in their despair or tossed off insults and told them to go back to where they came from.

I never once saw a Jesus brandishing a "Don't Tread On Me" bravado in the face of dire need.
I don't see him lecturing the poor and the afflicted to "pull yourselves up by your bootstraps."
I can't find him inviting war or celebrating bloodshed or reveling in loss of life for any reason.
I don't encounter him trolling those who express sadness or worry or struggle.
I don't see Jesus flipping defiant middle-finger contempt

towards those who came seeking refuge in him.
I see no arrogance that inflates his worth at the expense of someone else.

All of this is why I simply can't fathom Christians who are cruel; yet I see so many of them right now.

I watch them preaching and lecturing and hashtagging and boasting about winning, and I want to ask them, "But do you care about people?"

I'm not talking about the beliefs they profess or the policies they support or the values they claim to hold, but the manner in which they treat other human beings in the process—how they love or do not love their neighbor. I see countless proudly unloving people claiming to be Christians...and it's baffling.

If you profess to be a follower of Jesus, I'm not concerned with your politics and I don't care about your doctrine. I'm not interested in the Scriptures you can recite or the prayers you utter aloud. Show me a working theology of empathy. Show me that you actually give a damn about people—not just Republican people or American people or Christian people or white people—but the disparate parade of human beings in every way you encounter them, in every condition they arrive, with whatever backstory they've lived through.

If you tell me you're a Christian, be someone who—like Jesus—looks at the crowds and has a compassion for them that propels you into proximity with their pain.

Because if you aren't deeply burdened to live from a place of expansive, sacrificial, selfless love toward your neighbor; not moved to alleviate anguish or reduce suffering; not compelled to leave people better than you found them—honestly, I'm not sure what the point of calling yourself a Christian is.

That's what all my reading and prayer and ministering and living as a Christian have yielded: Following Jesus should leave me more compassionate, not less. It's really that simple.

As far as I can see, it's ridiculous to say I care about Jesus while not caring for the people placed in my path. I am called to live the greatest commandment, not to make any single nation "great."

I think most people walking the planet understand this, whether they're Christians or not.

They, too, get the gist of Jesus, and they see there is no bullying or malice or violence there. They recognize the disconnect between love and enmity when it shows up in their neighborhoods and on social media news feeds and in their living rooms—and they smell the putrid stench of hypocrisy a mile away.

I believe in a God of abundance. I can't comprehend a Christianity that sees others as in competition with me for jobs or healthcare or a home, because an infinite maker has infinite resources—and because I'm supposedly trying to emulate a Jesus who was the greatest expression *of* that abundance.

So maybe I'm wrong and maybe I need to regroup on this whole Christianity thing.

I thought we're supposed to care about people.

What am I missing?

# CHAPTER FOUR

# Dear Church, Here's Why People Are Leaving

Dear Church,

The exodus has begun and it's not going to stop.

People are leaving you and they're probably not coming back.

I've been where you are and I know what's happening within you right now.

I know you're panicking, scrambling to understand it all, trying to somehow stop the bleeding, to reverse the swift and steady tidal flow out the doors.

I know that you hire consultants and hold emergency meetings and plan bold strategies and brainstorm solutions—all designed to engineer a way to bring all the prodigals home, to "reach the young people," to grow numerically again.

I know you imagine that if you just tweak the songs or shorten the services or get a new sign or rebrand your logo or set up shop in a strip mall; that if you just find the right aesthetic balance of vintage reverence and hipster chic—this will all magically change your fortune.

It won't.

This attrition is likely irreversible and here's why:

The departure isn't about the style of music in your worship services.
It isn't about the coolness of the coffee shop facade in the lobby.
It isn't about the amenities you offer or can't offer.
It isn't about the tricked-out tech you're getting in the sanctuary.
It isn't about the youthfulness and charisma of your lead pastor.
It isn't about how many pop culture references you make in your sermons.
It isn't about the bells and whistles of your new website.
It isn't about your facilities or your staff or your social media fluency.
It isn't about the sprawling menu of ministries and Bible studies you offer.

The people who are gone aren't gone because your band wasn't good enough or because the messages weren't clever enough or because your production wasn't tight enough.

*They don't give a damn about such things.*

Church, people are leaving you because you are silent right now in ways that matter to them.

You aren't saying what they need you to say and what you should be saying—and it makes them sick.

They spend their days with a front row seat to human rights atrocities, to growing movements of cruelty, to unprecedented religious hypocrisy, and to political leaders who are antithetical to the heart of Jesus.

They live with the relational collateral damage of seeing people they love abandon compassion and decency—people who are growing more and more calloused to the already vulnerable.

They see in their daily lives and across their newsfeeds and on the news and in their communities *exactly* the kind of malevolence and toxicity they expect you to speak into with boldness and clarity as moral leaders—and instead they find you adjusting the stage lights and renovating the lobby and launching websites.

In the middle of the songs and the sermons and the video clips, they can see your feet of clay and your moral laryngitis. That's why they're leaving.

I know you're worried about saying too much, about being branded too political, about offending people, or somehow making it worse by speaking.

Trust me...you are making it worse by saying *nothing*.

Yes, you may be avoiding conflict or keeping a tenuous peace in the pews.

You may be causing less obvious turbulence inside your walls. You may be appeasing a few fearful folks there who don't want you to trouble the waters.

But you're doing something else: you're confirming for millions of people why they have no use for you any longer.

You're confirming the suspicions of those who believe the church has no relevance for them.

You're giving people who've offered you one more chance to earn their presence *reason to walk away.*

Your silence right now is the last straw for them.

They've been waiting for you to oppose the separation
of families,
to declare the value of black lives,
to loudly defend LGBTQ people,
to stand alongside your Muslim brothers and sisters,
to denounce the degradation of the planet—
to say with absolute clarity what you stand for and what you
will not abide.

And you have kept them waiting too long.

Church, people can get most of what you offer them somewhere else. They can find meaningful community and entertainment for their families and acts of service to complete. They can get music and inspiration and affinity and relationships without you.

The singular thing you can offer them is a clear and unflinching voice that emulates the voice of Jesus.

If you really want to be relevant again...*say everything*.

Stand on your platforms and in your pulpits and specifically name the bigotry, precisely call out the politics, unequivocally condemn the people and the policies and the movements that sicken you. Jesus did.

Stop couching your words and softening your delivery and start speaking with clarity about what matters to you. That's what those who are leaving want most.

It may be too late to stop the mass exodus at this point—but saying everything will at least help you keep your soul as they run away.

At least you'll know you stood for something.

Speak, Church.

# CHAPTER FIVE

# No, Being LGBTQ Is Not a Sin

Being gay is not a sin.

Neither is being lesbian, bisexual, or transgender.

The Bible never claims that it is.

It really doesn't.

Christians should stop saying that because it's reckless and irresponsible—and it's killing people.

It's the most reckless, wasteful, irresponsible misuse of religion; the most dangerous kind of stereotyping; the most lethal license to discriminate—and it's killing people who are made in the image of God.

Christians love to say that, by the way—that all human beings are "made in the image of God." Yet they also contend that these same *made-in-the-image-of-God human beings* are either created male *or* female; that any other non-binary expression of gender identity is against God's will; it's some unholy bastardization of the original plan.

The problem they have to deal with in declaring this is…God.

The oft-used line from the Genesis creation story actually quotes God as saying, "Let us make mankind in *our* image," and God then ultimately creates both men and women. If we are to take these words at face value—as so many homophobic/transphobic Christians do, we need to ask this question:

*Which ones were created in God's image: the males or the females?*

If our answer is *both*—which it must be—then God is decidedly non-binary; God transcends a single gender identity. God is by nature *trans*-gender. We cannot have God be a *male* and also make women in *His* image. We can't have a God capable of creating men *and* women unless God is equally made of both. These Christians wouldn't dream of excoriating God for the fluidity, would they?

These same folks also want to use the Bible to condemn LGBTQ people and to deny them the rights of marriage and church fellowship, but they have another problem: the Bible. They have all sorts of issues to contend with there.

Many Christians will attempt to use the word *homosexuality*—which does not occur in the original texts—as an umbrella term referring to both gender identity *and* sexual orientation. The context of the translated word they're using and the occasions it appears in Scripture, though, simply cannot refer to both things simultaneously. Additionally, many transgender people are, in fact, *not* same-sex oriented and not accurately described by the same word Christians would use to describe a gay or lesbian person.

They like to say that the Bible declares marriage to be strictly between *one man* and *one woman*. The Old Testament, though— as early as Genesis' fourth chapter—is teeming with bigamy, polygamy, and extra-martial sex practiced by the lauded pillars and patriarchs of the faith: Abraham, Gideon, Solomon, and David. Their stories are shared not as cautionary tales and not with rebuke, but simply as slices of the story of God's people. There are no definitive statements on marriage spanning the breadth of Scripture.

These Christians will frequently refer to the book of Leviticus, claiming it says that "homosexuality" is an *abomination* (a flawed talking point we'll discuss later) while ignoring surrounding verses commanding that disrespectful teens and those having extramarital sex be stoned to death. Hundreds of additional requirements and punishments in this text are declared irrelevant to their present lives. Current times have brought with them a highly selective use of the book of Leviticus.

These Christians will throw around the destruction of Sodom and Gomorrah as supposed proof of God's wrath against the gay community when, in fact, Ezekiel 16:49 declares that Sodom was destroyed because of its greed and disregard for the poor. But you don't see many of these Christians preaching that sermon, especially not GOP Christians.

These Christians will try to say that Jesus opposes the LGBTQ community when he *never once* corrects, cautions, or condemns anyone based on their gender identity or sexual orientation. In this case, we're supposed to believe the unspoken damnation is implied, when in reality these people are making Jesus say things he never said—simply because *they* want him to utter such words.

They'll refer to a "homosexual lifestyle" when the Bible is devoid of such terminology for the simple reason that the concept itself is ludicrous and nonexistent—as proven by the fact that a "heterosexual lifestyle" makes absolutely no sense when applied to straight people.

They'll claim that the term *homosexual* refers simply to people who have sex with same-gender partners, yet will also admit that their own *heterosexuality* refers to far more than just their sexual activity. It refers to their inclinations to love and where they seek affection, intimacy, and relationship. They can't have these words work both ways. They need to decide whether the less than a handful of passages in the New Testament are referring to identity, orientation, or a specific behavior by specific groups of people in a specific context—which is likely. Great unpacking of these passages is available here: https://www.gaychurch. org/homosexuality-and-the-bible/the-bible-christianity-and-homosexuality/.

These Christians will quote Paul in Romans Chapter 1, describing people consciously *"trading their natural attractions"* for same-sex desire and corresponding physical acts, failing to connect the dots that—for most members of the LGBTQ community—there is no such *exchanging* taking place. They aren't feeling one thing, and choosing an alternative simply to choose. They aren't acting in opposition to any primary inclination. Their same-sex orientation *is* their natural inclination. (If pressed, these Christians need to admit that this passage refers to a specific sex act tied to pagan worship practices, and cannot be superimposed over identity and orientation. And it's certainly not appropriate to use it to categorize committed, loving relationships by people along the full LGBTQ continuum.) When trying to use Paul's references in this way, they're trying to separate LGBTQ people from their capacity to love and be in mutually beneficial relationships...and that's simply wrong.

At the end of the day, the Bible is *not* clear on these matters. It is cloudy and even contradictory at times. There is no consistent sexual ethic in the Scriptures, no one image of marriage—and no specific condemnation from Jesus or Paul of those who are gay, lesbian, bisexual, or transgender *simply because of* their identity and orientation.

If we can admit that LGBTQ people have the same capacity for love, commitment, and monogamy in a mutually beneficial relationship that cisgender-heteronormative Christians do, biblical text becomes impossible to weaponize as it so often has been.

And the God of the Bible, as presented in Genesis, is himself/ herself/itself an image of the beautiful spectrum of sexuality, and a defense of those who believe we each manifest this complexity in a myriad of ways.

Christians wanting to persecute the LGBTQ community have long claimed that God and the Bible are their justifications. This simply isn't accurate, however, if they use the reality of God and all the words of the Bible rather than just the bits that feel like consent when isolated in social media diatribes and shouted sermons.

These people are going to have to admit that ultimately the only authority they're yielding to in these matters is their own... or that of the teachers or parents who have passed these ideas down to them. It is their fear, their prejudice, their lack of knowledge that causes them to lash out in hurtful words, violent rhetoric, and abject cruelty.

More and more Christians are beginning to understand this: Our faith tradition has gotten it wrong regarding sexuality the same way it has regarding the worth of women, the plague of slavery, interracial marriage, the violence against non-Christians, and on and on. They are seeing that being LGBTQ and being Christian are not mutually exclusive. They're seeing that a Church which honors God will welcome and *affirm* all people.

We've wasted so much time, so many resources, and so many beautiful, God-reflecting lives because we've made our fear our idol and tried to retrofit God into that image. The sooner we can let go of this misplaced fervor and this fruitless fight, the sooner we can live out Jesus' clear and unmistakable commands: we are to love God and all those who share this space with us.

No, being LGBTQ is not a sin.

The sin is the hatred that refuses to let go of that notion when evidence requires it.

# CHAPTER SIX

# The Religious Right Is Brainwashing People I Love

A year ago, I walked into the home of older relatives unannounced. We arrived thirty minutes earlier than we'd planned, but they were expecting us at lunchtime that day... so we knocked and walked in.

The small TV on the kitchen counter was playing Fox News.

When the wife came down the stairs, almost in the middle of greeting us, she walked hurriedly over to the sink, grabbed the remote, and turned off the TV—looking like a teenager watching porn getting caught by her parents.

Suddenly, everything made sense; all the dots connected.

During the last couple of years, I had noticed this couple changing but couldn't quite put my finger on it. They'd become more and more outspoken on things like immigration and women's reproductive rights and police shootings—surprising me with the intolerance and cruelty of off-the-cuff comments that seemed out of character for them. I questioned whether or not I was just being overly sensitive or projecting my fears onto them.

But after the surprise peek into their viewing habits, it was clear; they were just following the script.

I could rewind over the previous months and see all the alarmist Fox News talking points in their words at family gatherings and on Facebook: open borders letting in floods of rapists; baby-killing Democrats coming to take their guns; Muslim terrorists lurking everywhere; violent black men threatening police at traffic stops.

And looking back, I could see that just as they found Fox News, they began to lose their religion.

They no longer had much to say about Jesus—about his Matthew Chapter 25 promise that he would be found in "the least of these," and that we would be defined by the way we treat the poor and the vulnerable and the imprisoned.

They weren't interested in talking about the way he fed a hillside multitude of thousands—not because they earned it or deserved it, but because he was compassionate and they were hungry. They now just expressed disdain for lazy people wanting handouts.

They never referenced the fact that, while he was a newborn, Jesus' family fled to Egypt in desperation to escape politically-ordered genocide. Instead they preached about law-breaking families not "doing it the right way."

They abandoned any reference to Jesus' words about kindness or generosity or welcoming strangers or sharing what you had with those who had less. Instead, they slowly but quite clearly adopted a bastardized, angry, America First, gun-loving, immigrant-hating, racist white religion that has become the Republican God.

So whether it's anti-Muslim legislation or LGBTQ hate crimes or migrant kids taken from their parents, children orphaned by mass shooting, or a president fat-shaming protestors—there is always an excuse, always a justification, always a Fox News alternative reality or Franklin Graham tweet to bunker down in.

The same thing has happened in many of the white people I've served in churches here in the South over the last decade. Their social media feeds are increasingly littered with Brietbart fictional pieces about Hillary eating children and wild conspiracy theories about LGBTQ people converting their children.

The change in them has been stunning in its velocity and stomach-turning in its depths—and the worst part is that I can't reach them anymore. Before Fox News, Franklin Graham, and MAGA propaganda, I could meet them in the common ground of our shared faith in Jesus and in the clarity of objective truth. They no longer have use nor tolerance for such things.

The Sermon on the Mount—Jesus' counter-cultural, counterintuitive manifesto of humility and gentleness and love—has been replaced by venomous, incendiary Sean Hannity propaganda.

The barrier-breaking, table-expanding hospitality of Christ has morphed into sneering Trump rally rant rhetoric about violent illegals and foreign predators and "Build That Wall!" refrains.

These people used to know better. They were good-hearted, generous people who wanted to emulate Jesus. They used to flatly reject bigotry and defend vulnerable communities—and they were people I could count on for rational, level-headed decency.

They once instantly recognized men like Donald Trump as the antithesis of Jesus.

But this is what happens when decent, intelligent people become radicalized: They get polluted by the things they watch and the sermons they sit through and the nonsense they read. Then they surround themselves with an echo chamber made of equally deluded, equally frightened people—until one day, they are the religious extremists that they always used to warn you about.

I love my relatives, my former church members, my high school friends, and my neighbors—but I grieve what has happened to them. I lament the poisoning of their once soft hearts, and the way Jesus has been all but squeezed out of their religion. I fear that they'll never fully recover from the alternative narrative that these past three years have written into their brains about the world and about disparate people and about the expansive, lavish, audacious love Jesus calls us to extend.

I only hope these moms and ministers and nurses and schoolteachers and football coaches and favorite relatives get a truer story or meet someone who wakes them up or rediscover Jesus enough that they change the channel, turn off the TV— and find the truth that sets them free:

God is love.

We are our brother's keeper.

Kindness is the better path.

May it be so.

CHAPTER SEVEN

# The Christians Making Atheists

Growing up in the Church, I was taught that the worst thing one could be was a non-believer; that nothing was as tragic as a doomed soul that condemned itself by rejecting God. The religion of my childhood drew a sharp, clear line between the saved and the damned. All that mattered was making sure someone found themselves on the better side of this line— and the Atheists and Humanists didn't have a shot.

In light of this supposed truth, the heart of the faith (I was told) was to live in a way that reflected the character and love of Jesus so vividly, so beautifully, that others were compelled to follow after him; that a Christian's living testimony might be the catalyst for someone's conversion. The Bible called it "making disciples" and it was the heart of our tradition. As the venerable hymn declared, we Jesus people were to be known by our love.

What a difference a couple of decades makes.

Just ask around. People outside the Church will tell you: Love is no longer our calling card. It is now condemnation, bigotry, judgment, and hypocrisy. In fact, the Christianity prevalent in so much of America right now isn't just failing to draw others to Christ; it is actively repelling them from him. By operating in a way that is in full opposition to the life and ministry of Jesus, it is understandably producing people fully opposed to the faith that bears his name.

In record numbers, the Conservative American Church is consistently and surely making Atheists, or at the very least it is making *former* Christians—people who no longer consider organized religion an option because the Jesus they recognize is absent. With its sky-is-falling hand-wringing, its political bed-making, and its constant venom toward diversity, it is giving people no alternative but to conclude that, based on the evidence of people professing to be godly—God is of little use. In fact, this God may be toxic.

And that's the greatest irony of it all: The very Evangelicals who've spent that last 50 years in this country demonizing those who reject Jesus are now the single most compelling reason for them to do so. They are giving people who suspect that all Christians are self-righteous, hateful hypocrites all the evidence they need. The Church is confirming the outside world's most dire suspicions about this once most sacred institution.

These people aren't stupid. They realize that bigotry, even when it is wrapped in religion or justified by the Bible or spoken from a pulpit, is still bigotry. They can smell the putrid stench of phony religion from a mile away—and, frankly, this version of the Church reeks of it. People are steering clear in droves, choosing to find meaning and community and something that resembles love outside its gatherings.

With every persecution of someone in the LGBTQ community, with every unprovoked attack on Muslims, with every planet-wrecking decision, with every regressive civil rights move— the flight from Christianity continues. Meanwhile the celebrity preachers and professional Christians publicly beat their breasts about the multitudes walking away from God, oblivious to the fact that they are the impetus for the exodus.

And one day soon, these same religious folks will look around, lamenting the empty buildings and the irrelevance of the Church and a world that has no use for it, and they'll wonder how this happened. They'll blame a corrupt culture, or the liberal media, or a rejection of biblical values, or the devil himself—but it will be none of those things.

No, the reason the Church soon will be teetering on the verge of extinction and irrelevance will be because those entrusted to perpetuate the love of Jesus in the world lost the plot so horribly, and gave the world no other option but to look elsewhere for goodness and purpose and truth.

Soon these Evangelicals will ask why so much of America has rejected Jesus, and we will remind them of these days, and assure them that they have not rejected Jesus at all—they just found no evidence of him in them or their Church.

# CHAPTER EIGHT

# White Evangelicals, This Is Why People Are Through With You

Dear White Evangelicals,

I need to tell you something: People have had it with you.

They're done.

They want nothing to do with you any longer, and here's why:

They see your hypocrisy, your inconsistency, your incredibly selective mercy, and your thinly-veiled supremacy.

For eight years, they watched you relentlessly demonize a black president; a man faithfully married for 26 years; a doting father and husband without a hint of moral scandal or the slightest whiff of infidelity.

They watched you deny his personal faith convictions, argue his birthplace, and assail his character—all without cause or evidence. They saw you brandish Scriptures to malign him and use the laziest of racial stereotypes in criticizing him.

And through it all, White Evangelicals—you never once suggested that God placed *him* where he was:
You never publicly offered prayers for him and his family.
You never welcomed him to your Christian Universities.
You never gave him the benefit of the doubt in any instance.
You never spoke of offering him forgiveness or mercy.
Your evangelists never publicly thanked God for his leadership.
Your pastors never took to the pulpit to offer solidarity with him.
You never made any effort to affirm his humanity or show the love of Jesus to him in any quantifiable measure.

You violently opposed him at every single turn—without offering a single ounce of the grace you claim as the heart of your faith tradition. You jettisoned Jesus as you dispensed damnation on him.

And yet you give carte blanche to a white Republican man so riddled with depravity, so littered with extramarital affairs, so unapologetically vile, with such a vast resume of moral filth that the mind boggles.

And the change in *you* is unmistakable. It has been an astonishing conversion to behold: a being born again.

With him, you suddenly find religion.
With him, you're now willing to offer full absolution.
With him, all is forgiven without repentance or admission.
With him, you're suddenly able to see some invisible, deeply buried heart.
With him, sin has become unimportant, compassion no longer a requirement.
With him, you see only Providence.

And White Evangelicals, all those people who have had it with you? They see it all...clearly.

They recognize the toxic source of your inconsistency.
They see that pigmentation and party are your supreme deities.
They see that you aren't interested in perpetuating the love of God or emulating the heart of Jesus.
They see that you aren't burdened to love the least, or to be agents of compassion, or to care for your Muslim, gay, African, female, or poor neighbors as yourself.
They see that all you're really interested in doing is making a God in your own ivory image and demanding that the world bow down to it.
They recognize that this is all about white, Republican Jesus— not dark-skinned Jesus of Nazareth.

And I know you don't realize it, but you're digging your own grave these days—the grave of your very faith tradition.

Your willingness to align yourself with cruelty is a costly marriage. Yes, you've gained Supreme Court seats, a few years with the presidency as a mouthpiece, and the cheap high of temporary power—but you've lost a whole lot more.

You've lost an audience with millions of wise, decent, good-hearted, faithful people with eyes to see this ugliness.
You've lost any moral high ground or spiritual authority with an entire generation.
You've lost any semblance of Christlikeness.
You've lost the plot.
And most of all—you've lost your soul.

I know it's likely you'll dismiss these words. The fact that you've even made your bed with such malevolence shows how far gone you are and how insulated you are from the reality in front of you.

But I had to at least try to reach you. It's what Jesus would do.

Maybe you need to read what he said again—if he still matters to you.

Soon these Evangelicals will ask why so much of America has rejected Jesus, and we will remind them of these days, and assure them that they have not rejected Jesus at all—they just found no evidence of him in them or their Church.

CHAPTER NINE

# The Day I Chose My Heterosexuality

I still remember the day I chose to be heterosexual. It was when I was in fourth grade.

I was 10 years old and I already knew *all about* girls. I knew to take precautions with them. I knew to be very careful.

I knew they all had *girl germs*.

And if there's one thing a worldly young man like myself had already realized, it's that you definitely did *not* want to catch *girl germs*.

And so I spent every recess sprinting through the schoolyard, tearing around the jungle gym, and barreling through clusters of scattering kids—trying to escape being touched by any of the female runners. It was like the cornfield human round-up in the *Planet of the Apes* (or maybe *The Walking Dead*, a few decades earlier). I did my best to help the other boys when I could, of course, but we all knew that when push came to shove, it was every guy for himself. *Better them than me.*

We ran for our lives every lunchtime, knowing that to be touched was to be contaminated. But I was super fast. Maybe it was my sweet new pair of *Zips*, maybe it was my natural ability, or maybe it was adrenaline and desperation—but I was one heck of a runner.

That is...until Lori Kopcash.

Up until that day, Lori had been my greatest playground nemesis, and her very presence struck fear in my 10-year-old heart. She was gross and icky and absolutely *crawling with girl germs*—and she could run fast, too.

One afternoon, Lori was chasing me through the blur of the screaming crowd when I suddenly realized I wasn't running as fast as I could anymore. In fact, I was sort of dogging it on purpose. The truth blindsided me like a truck: something in me *really* wanted Lori Kopcash to catch me.

That was the day I *chose* my heterosexuality.

Of course, there was no real decision to be made here: no furious debate in my mind, no great wrestling with the choice at all. I simply became aware that Lori Kopcash made me feel something I'd never felt before. I couldn't rationalize it or explain it...I just liked her. I just liked girls. My perception of girls—and their respective germs—was never quite the same again.

We can all point to those moments early in our journey when we realize something true about how our hearts and bodies work. There would be more episodes of reckoning, but this was my first.

It wasn't until later that I learned, through the faith tradition I'd inherited, that apparently not all people worked this way. Some people, my Christianity told me, choose to be gay; they reject the very natural reality of what God has hard-wired into them; they make a conscious decision to be a *different* way. What I experienced without thinking on that playground—they somehow decide. What was an awareness for me was, for them, a premeditated choice.

I knew right away how ridiculous an idea that was.

I knew that it was both arrogant and ignorant to imagine that anyone else's experience of attraction or affection or desire was any different from mine—simply because their attraction, affection, and desire experiences were oriented differently. The story that my religion told me about these things just didn't ring true that day. It still doesn't.

Later, when I became a pastor, I was committed to remembering how natural what I felt that afternoon for Lori felt, and to work toward a Church that respects the idea that we each have a truest truth; that we should be allowed to live and love and worship from that most authentic place. If God made *any* of us to naturally feel what we feel without getting to choose it—God created *all* of us this way.

One of the greatest failings I see in my fellow Christians is assuming that they can determine what is natural for someone else—the *real* of the other, the *truth* of the other—that they can decide for another person who *they* are.

It grieves me when I see followers of Jesus dismissing someone else's story: their sense of identity, their inclination to love, the orientation of their affections, and the revelation of their own hearts. It is as if these followers of Jesus know more about those people than they know about themselves; It's the height of hubris.

One of the prayers I carry daily is that more people who claim faith in Jesus will find the humility to remember what they learned about themselves at some point in their lives, and to allow everyone the dignity of coming to their own conclusions.

There, on the playground of St. Mary's Catholic School, Lori Kopcash made me stop running. And when I did, I woke up to the way my heart worked. I didn't choose anything; I discovered it.

These are two gifts we should give everyone—both inside and outside the Church: the joy of celebrating who they really are, and the trust that they are best equipped to tell and live out their own stories.

We should tell all people that when it comes to how they love and who they love...they can stop running.

# CHAPTER TEN

# Being Ghosted for My Heresy by MAGA Christians

People often say God moves in mysterious ways.

I won't argue with them.

I've been a local church pastor for more than two decades. Over recent years, as I started to ask more questions and as my faith grew more and more progressive, I faced a massive exodus of friends and family.

I lost hundreds, perhaps thousands of former church friends and co-ministers who disconnected, went silent, or actively ridiculed me for "falling away from the faith."

A former pastor publicly disparaged me for losing my way. Longtime Christian friends ghosted me, avoiding eye contact at stores and at funerals for mutual friends. I now get the cold shoulder on social media from people I used to live and work alongside; they're using their silence to teach me a lesson about my heresy.

Since the exodus, I've watched many of these same people move lock-step with this completely immoral president, and betray nearly everything about the life and ministry of Jesus—like Peter repeatedly denying him in the garden before his arrest and murder.

They've said they love their neighbor as themselves—but have gone all-in with Muslim bans and ICE raids and bathroom bills and healthcare repeals.
They have loudly contested the mattering of black lives, while claiming to desire a "diverse church."
They've preached about "God so loving the world," and yet passionately declared "America First."
They have defended comments about "shithole countries," where we served together on life-altering short-term mission trips.

It has been a sickening marvel to witness the hypocrisy of men and women for whom I was no longer "Christian enough" (because I welcomed LGBTQ people or questioned the existence of Hell or the inerrancy of Scripture) suddenly justify sexual predators, ignore porn star affairs, applaud the building of walls, celebrate the silencing of black athletes, and cheer the separation of families.

The same Christians who shunned me for reminding them that Jesus wasn't white, American, or Christian essentially became vocal activists solely for white American Christians.

But these days have been uniquely and tragically illuminating.

I've seen many of the professed Christians for whom my progressive faith expression was problematic witness the horrors unfolding at our border and say absolutely nothing.
They have been silent and still while hell has broken loose—and I've noticed.

As has happened so many times over the past two years, I'm reminded of Jesus' words that whatever we do to the "least of these"—those disregarded and vulnerable and helpless—we do to him. I look at the people who severed ties with me and I realize how glad I am to be where I am and not where they are.

I realize that whatever the personal cost of my perceived heresy has been in relationship disconnection, it's been worth it because it's given me an empathy that, for whatever reason, now eludes them. It has given me a clear voice where they now have moral laryngitis. Their rejection has pushed me to a more expansive space, to a much larger table. Moving away from their religion, I think I've found closer proximity to Jesus.

As much as I've grieved the loss of these people and have been wounded by their condemnation and judgment, I'm grateful that I am in a different place in my spiritual journey.

I'll take my divergence from the "right path" and deep compassion for hurting people over orthodoxy and a hardened heart any day.
I'll gladly take my place outside of their approval, and alongside

children being brutalized and the weary seeking refuge.
I'll gratefully accept their sentence of damnation in the afterlife
if it means I live this life giving a damn about people who
are hurting.
I'll make my home here with the rest of the heretics, apostates,
backsliders, and sinners—and with a Jesus my former friends
no longer recognize as in their midst.

I once was blind, but now I see.

# CHAPTER ELEVEN

# The Church Beloved: A Manifesto of LGBTQ-Affirming Christians

A new Church is coming! Or rather, with each passing day, it is *becoming*—person by person being renovated.

Heart by heart, it is waking up.

For a long time we have been shamed into silence, relegated to the periphery of the faith community, believing in quiet. But these days demand volume, and today we raise our voices so that there can be no mistaking our intentions.

We are unrepentantly, unwaveringly LGBTQ-affirming Christians.

We will continue to make the Church and this world a more open, loving, and safe place for the LGBTQ community and their families.

We believe the Church must be fully inclusive in both the pews and the pulpit, or it is less in the image of God than it could and should be.

We believe that gender identity and sexual orientation have no bearing on a person's moral worth or their standing in the eyes of God.

We believe we are all beloved as we are...without alteration.

We believe that everyone is a reflection of the Divine, created good, made of what God is made of.

We believe Jesus calls us to love one another, not to tolerate one another; not to warmly embrace some and to hold others at a distance.

We celebrate all life with equal ferocity.

We're not going to apologize for any of this and we're not relenting.

We're not stopping because our faith compels *us*, just as your faith compels you.

We, too, have read the Bible and gone to seminary and served in the Church and prayed fervently and listened intently for the voice of God, and all of these things have yielded our conclusions.

We will gladly tell you why we believe what we believe, but we're not going to argue with you about the validity of our convictions because we don't need to justify our path to you.

We've already walked our road.

We understand that, because of what you believe, our position may cause fear and anger to rise up and boil over, and that you may feel the need to defend yourself. You may feel driven to attack us, sometimes violently, and we will try to respond... not in kind, but in kindness.

We will do our best to reflect the Jesus we have come to know by not questioning your humanity or your character or the legitimacy of your faith—but we will also continue to speak without censoring or softening, because refraining from that is how injustice is allowed to fester and spread.

You can say all manner of hateful, disparaging, insulting things, but that doesn't matter, because we believe in the inherent worth of all people and we believe that Scripture bears this out.

We will no longer tolerate a Church where any group of people is marginalized in the name of God and we will speak into that with sustained force.

To say it plainly—We're here for the duration, so shouting us down or shutting us off is not a viable option.

A Church without the LGBTQ community is simply no longer acceptable and we, Christians of all identities and orientations, stand together to speak in unison:

*Love is indeed winning and we are the loud and shimmering proof.*

If this is bad news to you, we're going to refer you to Jesus and let the two of you work it out. We don't believe we can change you anyway. God does the changing.

In the meantime, we're going to keep living our faith convictions just as you live yours, and we're going to love people as God personally calls us to.

This is how that "freedom in Christ" thing works.

We are the Church that is becoming what it was meant to be: fully, unapologetically inclusive.

We are the Church Beloved.

CHAPTER TWELVE

# Why Do You Stand Behind Cruelty?

You are a mystery to me.

I watch you standing there with wide-eyed, breathless adoration, and I simply can't fathom how you ended up there in that spot; what it is you're feeling in that moment; how *this* has become a voice with which you feel affinity.

Why are you here?

I'd never stand behind someone who makes fun of stutterers.

I'd never stand behind someone who uses a person's physical appearance as a slur.

I'd never stand behind someone who speaks about women as though they are things.

I'd never stand behind someone who mocks people with disabilities.

I'd never stand behind someone who exploits racial and ethnic stereotypes.

I'd never choose such a person as a friend, let alone choose them to make decisions regarding hundreds of millions of people or to represent me in the world or to shape the place my children call home—and the reason has nothing at all to do with politics.

It's a human decency thing.

I'd never do these things, because as a Christian I was raised to treat people with a dignity that I was taught they deserve as solely unique human beings, fearfully and wonderfully made in the image of a God who was Love.

I was raised to believe that I was fortunate to be born where I was born with the advantages I have and surrounded by the love I was surrounded by and inside the healthy body I inhabited; and that I should remember many people were not—and that this makes life more difficult for them.

I was raised to look for the uncomfortable people on the periphery and to welcome them in: to make them feel seen and heard, to reduce the loneliness they experience, to help them feel less isolated than they usually do.

I was taught to defend bullied people, to befriend the vulnerable, and to extend kindness in a way that makes someone else's load lighter—because life is heavy and it's difficult on its best day.

I was taught that compassion is the better path...or in plain language, not to be a jerk.

What were you taught that was so different?

I also grew up knowing that you can't believe one thing while saying another; that your actions ultimately declare what you value despite what you claim to value with words; that if your personal faith is never tangibly embodied in your daily life— it is simply a showy, dressed up corpse.

As an adult, I've interpreted this to mean that your politics reveal who you are: that you vote for people you agree with, who reflect your heart, who share your values, who speak for you—people who in some significant way embody you.

When you hear him speak, how can you identify as a kindred spirit?

Our politics aren't some detached entities that exist apart from our moral convictions and our personal values; rather, our politics are direct extensions of them. We choose human beings to represent us in the world—those who do and say what we would do and say if we had the power and position they have.

I really wonder why you've chosen this man to speak for you.

I wonder what about the slurs and the taunts and the nicknames and the expletives and the viciousness feels congruent with the way you see the world.

I wonder what vicarious impulse you express through him when he provokes people he has power over, especially when they are at their most vulnerable.

I wonder how the continual stream of vengeful attacks on already marginalized communities gives voice to something you harbor in the deepest recesses of your heart.

I wonder why this hatred is something with which you feel solidarity.

You tell me you're not a mean-spirited person, that you don't harbor hatred in your heart, that you have no desire to see people hurt, and I want to believe you—but this alliance is a serious disconnect.

For some reason, you stand proudly behind cruelty.

You cheer it on when it generates pain for people.

You laugh when it makes jokes at the expense of others' misery.

You "Amen!" its ever-lowering bottom.

You applaud when it strains wildly to outdo itself in falsehoods.

What does it say about your understanding of Jesus?

What does it echo about the way you see people?

What does it say about the fear that you fight every day to push back?

What does it reveal about the value you see in those who don't look or speak or love or believe the way you do?

Try as I might, I simply can't understand it from where I am.

Tell me why you stand behind cruelty.

# CHAPTER THIRTEEN

# Dear LGBTQ Children, God Adores You

Today our daughter came home from school and told us about a classmate who wore a shirt from her church. It said:

God

Adores

You

One of the students noticed the first letters of each word spelled out the word "GAY" and started to make fun of her.

Based on the girl's response, the shirt wasn't designed to broadcast that message, and she was both surprised and embarrassed by the revelation of the unintended statement.

After some uncomfortable words, the boy later apologized and they all went on with their day, seemingly smoothing everything over as young children are able to do.

I wondered what the after-school conversation at home was like for the girl and her family. I wondered if this was the first time the "mistake" had been discovered by the church; if there would be a hastily-called emergency meeting with panic-stricken parents, followed by massive recalls or shirt burnings.

More than that, I thought about young LGBTQ people in schools throughout the country who are taunted and laughed at and excluded every day for simply existing—often by hateful people professing belief in a God who is Love. During an already vulnerable time where they are already feeling isolated from their peers, their worth is regularly called into question and their identity assailed—and they often don't get an apology and immediate restoration. They don't get to simply be and be loved.

I hate that any child would be bullied over who they were, or were even *suspected* of being—but there was something revelatory about the possibility of a Christian family experiencing the kind of cruelty that Christians continually dispense toward people based on their gender identity or sexual orientation. I wonder if the irony of the moment registered.

I'm grateful for the inadvertent LGBTQ affirmation from a church, and I hope the people who designed it consider explicitly speaking that message and begin to reexamine how big God's love actually is—if God is God-sized.

Followers of Jesus are supposed to be walking billboards of that radical affection for everyone. That's what he meant by *being the light* to a world that can be very dark for so many. We need more light-bringers these days.

I'd love to see Christians intentionally declaring the value of *all* people more often—that they'd step proudly and loudly into their classrooms and workplaces and family gatherings, wearing this message on their sleeves: *Everyone is beloved as they arrive here; they are fiercely loved without caveat or condition.*

They say the LORD works in mysterious ways, so why not through a cotton/poly blend and some glitter paint?

To all my LGBTQ friends out there who daily face the taunts and the threats and the coldness of people claiming faith in a God who is supposed to be made of love...please accept my apologies for them wielding religion like a weapon. They know not what they do.

And as you study and work and play and live in this world, please remember that—regardless of what anyone tells you on signs or on shirts or in sermons—

Be greatly encouraged.

You are fearfully and wonderfully made—and God adores you.

CHAPTER FOURTEEN

# This Isn't Christianity

*"And when you pray, do not be like the hypocrites, for they love to pray standing in the synagogues and on the street corners to be seen by others. Truly I tell you, they have received their reward in full. But when you pray, go into your room, close the door and pray to your Father, who is unseen. Then your Father, who sees what is done in secret, will reward you."—Jesus (Matthew 5:5-6)*

*"You keep using that word. I do not think it means what you think it means."—Inigo Montoya (The Princess Bride)*

We need to be really clear on something, because there seems to be confusion out there lately:

*This isn't Christianity.*

They may use the word and steal the iconography and cop the aesthetic, but that is where the resemblance diverges and where the similarities end. There remain no other commonalities with which to rightly associate the two.

*This isn't Christianity.*

It is spiritual misappropriation: weaponizing the violent hijacking of something helpful in order to do the greatest amount of damage in the shortest amount of time; hostiley taking over something beautiful, and grossly disfiguring it to terrorize people.

*This isn't Christianity*—at least not what Jesus intended it to be.

Jesus intended Christianity to look like this:

*"Blessed are the poor in spirit, for theirs is the kingdom of heaven.*

*Blessed are those who mourn, for they will be comforted.*

*Blessed are the meek, for they will inherit the earth.*

*Blessed are those who hunger and thirst for righteousness, for they will be filled.*

*Blessed are the merciful, for they will be shown mercy.*

*Blessed are the pure in heart, for they will see God.*

*Blessed are the peacemakers, for they will be called children of God."*

—*Jesus (Matthew 5:3-10)*

And there is nothing of mercy or humility or purity or peacemaking in this thing claiming to be Christianity.

No, this thing is the antithesis of all of it.

*This isn't Christianity*—at least, not if we're going to listen to Jesus.

Where Jesus implored Christians to love and to care for and to show hospitality to their neighbors—this drives people to fear them and have contempt for them and send them back and wall them off.

Where Jesus directed Christians to pray and to give in quiet and secret—this is a shameless, staged photo op to engender applause.

Where Jesus told Christians that they would be defined by the way in which they lavishly love humanity—this is a malicious assault on nearly all of it.

Where Jesus directed Christians to live humbly and take the lowest place—this is arrogance and boasting and self-promotion.

Where Jesus fed multitudes and healed the sick without asking for repayment—this is healthcare repeals and canceled school lunch programs and "pull yourself up by your own bootstraps" disdain for the needy.

Where Jesus' followers shared all things and lived interdependently and made sure that no one went without—this is cries of "Socialism" whenever those with abundance are asked to share with those who lack.

Where Jesus threw open the doors of the kingdom so that the entire world could find welcome and refuge and comfort—this is a guarded, gated community of privileged, close-fisted white Americans.

*No, this isn't Christianity*—and more people who know what Christianity was intended to be need to say so right now.

We need to call this what it is: a bait and switch of the vilest kind.

This may be what Franklin Graham says Christianity is.
It may be what Paula White wants you to believe Christianity is.
It may be what Bible Belt pastors screaming from their pulpits claim that Christianity is.
It may be what Donald Trump wants to pretend that Christianity is.
It may be what it has been too many times in the past two thousand years, when opportunistic hucksters like these have commandeered it.

It's just not what Jesus says it is.

No, he told us what *this* is:

*"Watch out for false prophets. They come to you in sheep's clothing, but inwardly they are ferocious wolves. By their fruit you will recognize them. Do people pick grapes from thorn bushes, or figs from thistles? Likewise, every good tree bears good fruit, but a bad tree bears bad fruit. A good tree cannot bear bad fruit, and a bad tree cannot bear good fruit. Every tree that does not bear good fruit is cut down and thrown into the fire. Thus, by their fruit you will recognize them."—Jesus (Matthew 7:15-20)*

*This thing is not Christianity.*

Jesus said it wasn't.

This is Rome.
This is the Empire.

This is corrupt and predatory power.

This is a perverted religion wielded like a hammer.

This is hypocritical, showy piety paraded for everyone to see.

This is the darkness Jesus claimed we should streak into as brilliant lights.

This is the bloated ugliness he said we were to oppose by living quietly and gently.

This is the table of greed he invited us to angrily turn over.

The Christianity of Jesus left people with more dignity and greater care; with healed wounds and fuller bellies; with calmed fears and quieted worries. It left people seen and heard and known. It left a wake of kindness and generosity and goodness and compassion.

No, this isn't Christianity.

To Hell with what *this* is.

# CHAPTER FIFTEEN

# The Kind of Christian I Refuse to Be

I am a Christian.

Actually, lately it's more accurate to say that I am *still* a Christian.

I now say this with much trepidation. I say it with great fatigue. I say it somewhat begrudgingly. I say it with more than a good deal of embarrassment—not about Jesus, but about so many of his people and so much of the Church professing to speak for him.

Seeing too much negativity and hatred in what now represents my faith tradition, it's become a daily battle to make this once effortless declaration. I know that it now automatically aligns me with those who share so little in common with the Jesus I met when I first claimed the name *Christian*.

I know the immediate response people likely have when I make this declaration; I know the kind of people they associate me with in an instant.

*I am a Christian* now aligns me with bathroom bullies, politicized pulpits, white privilege, and overt racism; with bigotry toward so many groups of people who represent the *world* I grew up believing that *God so loved*.

There are things that used to be givens, absolutes when one made a claim to follow Jesus. They no longer seem to be.

For far too many people, being a Christian no longer means you need to be humble or forgiving. It no longer means you need a heart to serve or to bring healing. It no longer requires compassion or mercy or benevolence. It no longer requires you to turn the other cheek or to love your enemies or to take the lowest place or to love your neighbor as yourself.

It no longer requires *Jesus*.

And so the choices are to abandon the idea of claiming Christ altogether to avoid being deemed *hateful by association* in the eyes of so much of the watching world—or to reclaim the name Christian so that it once again replicates the love of Jesus in the world.

I am trying to do the latter.

Yes, I am a Christian, but there is a Christian I refuse to be.

*I refuse to be a Christian who lives in fear of people who look or speak or worship differently than I do.*

*I refuse to be a Christian who believes that God blesses America more than God so loves the world.*

*I refuse to be a Christian who can't find the beauty and truth in religious traditions other than my own.*

*I refuse to be a Christian who uses the Bible to perpetuate individual or systemic bigotry, racism, or sexism.*

*I refuse to be a Christian who treasures allegiance to a flag or a country or a political party above emulating Jesus.*

*I refuse to be a Christian who is reluctant to call out the words of hateful preachers, venomous politicians, and mean-spirited pew sitters in the name of keeping ceremonial Christian unity.*

*I refuse to be a Christian who tolerates a global Church where all people are not openly welcomed, fully celebrated, and equally cared for.*

*I refuse to be a Christian who always speaks with holy war rhetoric about an encroaching enemy horde that must be rallied against and defeated.*

*I refuse to be a Christian who is generous with damnation and stingy with Grace.*

*I refuse to be a Christian who can't see the image of God in people of every color, every religious tradition, every sexual orientation.*

*I refuse to be a Christian who demands that others believe what I believe or live as I live or profess what I profess.*

*I refuse to be a Christian who sees the world in a hopeless downward spiral and can only condemn it or withdraw from it.*

*I refuse to be a Christian devoid of the character of Jesus: his humility, his compassion, his smallness, his gentleness with people's wounds, his attention to the poor and the forgotten and the marginalized, his intolerance for religious hypocrisy, his clear expression of the love of God.*

*I refuse to be a Christian unless it means I live as a person of hospitality, of healing, of redemption, of justice, of expectation-defying Grace, of counterintuitive love. These are non-negotiables.*

Yes, it is much more difficult to say it these days than it has ever been, but I still do say it.

I am *still* a Christian—but I refuse to be one without Jesus.

.

PART TWO

# Stuff That Needs To Be Said About America, Race, and Politics

CHAPTER SIXTEEN

# I'm Not the Radical Left; I'm the Humane Middle

Apparently, I've been radicalized and I wasn't aware.

Certain people call me the "Radical Left" all the time.

I never considered myself radical before.

I thought I was just normal, ordinary, usual.

I thought equity was important to everyone.

I imagined America was filled with people who took that Life, Liberty, and Pursuit of Happiness stuff seriously—for all people.

I thought the Golden Rule was actually mainstream.

Recently I took an inventory of my positions, screening for the extremism:

I believe in full LGBTQ rights.

I believe we should protect the planet.

I believe everyone deserves healthcare.

I believe all religions are equally valid.

I believe the world is much bigger than America.

I believe to be "pro-life" means to treasure its entire spectrum.

I believe whiteness isn't superior—that it is not the baseline
of humanity.

I believe we are all one interdependent community.

I believe people and places are made better by diversity.

I believe people shouldn't be forced to abide by anyone
else's religion.

I believe non-American human beings have as much value as
American ones.

I believe generosity is greater than greed, compassion better
than contempt, and kindness superior to derision.

I believe there is enough in this world for everyone: enough food,
enough money, enough room, enough care—if we unleash our
creativity and unclench our fists.

I'm not sure how these ideas became radical, though that is
exactly what seems to have happened in the last few years.

I grew up being taught that these principles and positions were
just part of being a decent human.

I grew up believing that loving my neighbor as myself meant that
I actually worked for his or her welfare as much as my own.

I was taught that caring for the least in the world was a measure
of my devotion to God.

I thought that acknowledging and respecting inalienable rights
of other people were supposed to be priorities of decent citizens
of the world.

I don't think I'm alone.

In fact, I'm pretty sure that most people residing in this place alongside me have the desire for compassion and diversity and equality and justice for all; that these things aren't fringe ideologies or extremist positions—but simply the best way to be human.

I think most people want more humanity, not less.

I think the vast middle is exhausted by the cruelty of these days.

That these aspirations seem radical to some people is probably an alarm that they've moved so far into the extremes of their fortified ideological bunkers and have been so poisoned by the propaganda that normal now seems excessive. Equality now seems oppressive; goodness now feels reckless.

Maybe the problem is that these people are so filled with fear for those who are different, so conditioned to be at war with the world, so indoctrinated into a white nationalistic religion of malice—that they've lost sight of what decent humanity looks like anymore.

I am pretty sure that I don't represent the "Radical Left," but the vast, disparate, compassionate, humane middle: people who are not threatened by someone else's presence, who do not see another person's gain as their loss, who don't worship a Caucasian, American god.

I suppose humanity feels radical to inhumane people.

In that case, I'll gladly be here in my extremism.

# CHAPTER SEVENTEEN

# America's Greatest Threat Isn't Migrant or Muslim

The President spends a great deal of time telling Americans how frightened they should be of the people walking among them.

He reminds them every chance he gets that there are some "very bad" people in their midst: people who threaten their safety, people with little regard for the law, people who believe the law doesn't apply to them.

I wholeheartedly agree with him. There *is* a clear and present danger in these times.

There *are* people here that decent Americans should be terrified by who have gained traction and are growing in numbers and ferocity—but they're not exactly those the president wants to conveniently paint as the danger.

I see them, though.

Yesterday, while in a busy beach town, a car came flying in from behind us in heavy stop and go traffic.

The driver was a young white man. As he sped past us, I noticed that he had bumper stickers that read, "Fight Crime: Shoot Back" and "No Liberals."

Not surprising, he drove aggressively—weaving back and forth, tailing cars close behind, then shooting around them. His face was etched in a permanent scowl, and he seemed bothered by the whole lot of humanity surrounding him. I've seen that look before, but I see it a lot more lately.

As I watched the man rev his engine and furrow his brow, I realized that Donald Trump is right: there *are* emboldened bad people who are sapping America of its greatness.

I rarely feel any angst about people coming across our borders or from other countries—and I certainly don't worry for my children's safety because of them. I seldom witness violence, never see them try to intimidate the people around them, and have never once seen such people committing hate crimes against other Americans.

I'm never uneasy about Muslims or undocumented people or migrant families passing me on the street.

No—it's pissed-off, entitled, gun-toting, professed Christian white bigots emboldened by this president who terrify me.

They're the ones pulling the triggers in most of our
mass shootings.
They're the ones accosting strangers because of their sexuality
or skin color.
They're the ones trolling teenage mass shooting survivors.
They're the ones espousing the most toxic of religions.
They're the ones carrying torches through cities and ramming
people with cars.
They're the ones most often using excessive force behind badges.
They're the ones feeling they now have license to say anything
they'd like.
They're the ones calling the cops on black men sitting in
coffee shops.
They're the ones who believe America is solely their property
and birthright.
They're the ones most emboldened by this president, in whom
they've found a kindred spirit.

I am far more afraid for my children around people like these than the fantastical caricatures or statistically nonexistent boogeymen the president is trying to make out of brown-skinned people from other countries.

I am fully terrified by racism, homophobia, Islamophobia, and all the other supremacy sicknesses being cultivated right now in the hearts of white Americans by a fraudulent leader who knows that this is his only play.

So yes, Donald Trump is absolutely correct: America *is* in danger—danger that is homegrown and being replicated by those in power, most especially the president. It is a danger that feeds on fear, thrives on nationalism, and believes our heritage to be oppressed.

Yes, we who live and work and make our homes here—those who represent the beautiful, radiant diversity of this country—need to resist the violence asserting itself here right now.

We need to condemn the language and the people and the systems that incubate, protect, and foster this kind of hatred.

The real threat to our nation's safety is an inside job. It didn't need to cross our borders.

It is already at home here.

I suppose humanity feels radical to inhumane people.

In that case, I'll gladly be here in my extremism.

# CHAPTER EIGHTEEN

# Trump-Supporting Friend—This Isn't About Donald Trump

Trump-supporting friend,

What we've got here is failure to communicate…

I know you think I'm preoccupied with this president; that *he* is the reason I'm so angry and bitter and frustrated these days—but you're wrong.

This isn't about Donald Trump.

It's never been about him.

It wasn't about him during the campaign or on Election Day.
It wasn't about him when recordings of him boasting about sexual assaults surfaced.
It wasn't about him when he said protestors at campaign rallies should be roughed up.
It wasn't about him when he left refugee families stranded at the airport.
It wasn't about him when he attacked the press.
It wasn't about him when he sabotaged the Affordable Care Act.
It wasn't about him when he blamed racial violence on "both sides."

And it isn't about him today: It's about *us*.

This is about *me* and it's about *you*.

It's about my grief at the ugliness you feel emboldened to post on social media now; the nastiness you seem capable of now; the disgusting words you so easily toss out around the dinner table now.

It's about my disbelief at your sudden tolerance for his infidelity, his cruelty, his intellectual ignorance, his immorality, his disrespect for the rule of law, his alliances with dictators—things you once claimed you could never abide in a leader.

It's about my incredulity at your surprising resentment for marginalized people; for your inability to muster any compassion for those who are hurting or frightened or threatened.

It's about my disappointment at your easily manipulated nationalistic fervor; how the *God and Guns, America First, Love it or Leave it* rhetoric so easily took root in your heart—how hostile to outsiders and foreigners you've become.

It's about my amazement at your capacity to make your faith so pliable that you could "Amen!" a compulsive liar, a serial adulterer, a fear-mongering bully; a man in nearly every way antithetical to the Jesus you've always said was so dear to you.

It's about my sickness seeing you excuse away his coddling of racists, his public attacks on the FBI, his impulsive firings of Cabinet members, his Tweet rants against individual citizens and American companies.

It's about my grief at seeing you respond to his near-hourly display of recklessness and overreach with a shrug of your shoulders or a turning away from it all.

It's about me watching you ignore in him and even celebrate in him the very things you claimed made Hillary Clinton the "greater of two evils" when you voted in 2016: blatant corruption, financial impropriety, pathological lies, lack of morality.

It's about my sadness at seeing you make a million tiny concessions—and how easy it now is for you to consent to actions that, only three years ago, you'd have told me fully disgusted you.

Most of all, it's about me realizing that when all this is over— we are still going to have to deal with the fallout from it all. Our fractures are going to outlive this presidency.

You see, I really *don't* give a damn about Donald Trump.

He doesn't matter to me. He never has.

He's a three-time married, C-level Reality TV celebrity with a long and well-documented resume of sexual misconduct, financial disasters, and moral filth. He's a professional predator who's spent his life exploiting people for personal gain. That's who he was before and who he will be when he leaves office.

Donald Trump, the president, will be gone one day and his disastrous presidency will be well-preserved. History will have documented his every lie, every misdeed, every abuse of power, every treasonous betrayal—and he will be fully revealed as the monster that many of us are fully aware he is.

That's not why I am so disgusted and so filled with sadness these days.

I don't care about Donald Trump because I don't know or live alongside or love or respect Donald Trump.

I know and live alongside and love and respect *you*—or at least I once did, and I'm going to have to try to do that again.

Our relationships and our families and our churches and our neighborhoods and our nation are going to be cleaning up the messes long after this president is gone.

When this is all over, the divides and the fractures and the wounds between us are going to remain.

This is why I'm angry and bitter and frustrated; not because of Donald Trump—but because of me—and because of you.

# CHAPTER NINETEEN

# The Political Extinction of the White American Male Dinosaur

I love the look I saw this week.

It was the look of terrified dinosaurs realizing that the meteorite is on its way; the dilated pupils in the eyes of leadened, lumbering prehistoric monsters who've had their run of the house, now finding themselves at the precipice of political extinction.

The most diverse Congress in our history began its 2019 session as a harbinger of what is coming for this nation, and what this means for their species. America is growing more diverse, and its representative leadership, though still painfully lagging behind, is quickly making up ground. They can see the change in the weather and the light in the sky—and they are scrambling to avoid the coming impact because they can sense it will not end well for them.

It's why Mitch McConnell is holding the government hostage over an ineffective, multi-billion dollar monument to the racism of a border wall that two-thirds of this country doesn't want.
It's why men like Tucker Carlson rant mindlessly about successful women ushering in the "decline of men."
It's why Jim Mattis and Michael Cohen and General Kelly and Mike Flynn and a perpetually revolving door of men are leaving or being forced out of positions of influence and leadership.
It's why Republican leaders have spent the past year creating a massive straw man out of exhausted migrant families and refugee children, as though they were wealthy foreign adversaries rigging a presidential election.
It's why right-wing trolls "leaked" a video of a college-aged Alexandria Ocasio-Cortez dancing, as if it was a clip of her saying she could grab less powerful men by the genitalia.
It's why Liberty University President Jerry Falwell, Jr. performed embarrassingly contorted theological gymnastics in order to align with this president over poor people.
It's why Donald Trump spent Christmas Eve bunkered down in the White House behind a smartphone, tweeting scattered, rapid-fire nonsense—instead of being with his family or reading or, God forbid, serving someone.

It is the white-hot fear that has overtaken them all.

They're all in a scalding panic because they understand that their brief moment in history to have their way and impose their will is quickly coming to a close. The landscape is being renovated, the climate is changing, and, as a species, they are dying—which is why they will do what all frightened animals do when they are backed into a corner and realize the level of the threat: they will grow more violent than ever before.

In the coming days, the Tweets will become more erratic; the legislative assaults will grow more transparently desperate; the hate crimes more brazen; the sermons more alarmist and incendiary. These Jurassic, soon-to-be-amber-trapped relics will act as if the very sky above them is falling because, in very real ways, it is. They will thrash and spit and bellow in an effort to buy themselves a few more days and a bit more power and another federal judge or two—but they cannot stave off their inevitable political disappearance, as progress and civilization and time swallow them up.

The misogynistic, supremacist nostalgia of their dying glory days is dissolving in the glorious refining fire of what is coming on the horizon: Color and diversity and new and young and wide open. The wall-builders and the close-fisted and the table-monopolizers will not survive this evolution.

America's history is being rewritten in real-time by a fearless, disparate, interdependent humanity of every creed and orientation and nation of origin, and despite a reign that seemed like it would never end, the once mighty white dinosaurs are running out of real estate—and time.

Their eyes tell the story.

They see extinction coming.

We all do.

# CHAPTER TWENTY

# Yes World, It's That Bad Here in America— and Worse

A reader from Australia texted me last night. He'd been watching the news and said he wanted to check on me.

*We're heartbroken to hear what's going on there,* he wrote. *Is it really as bad as it looks?*

Another sweet friend from England messaged me this morning with similar concern for me and for our nation, based on what she's been reading and seeing in the media.

Over the past few weeks, I've had many kind-hearted people from all over the world make similar inquiries about America...

asking if it is as dire and alarming up close as it appears from a distance.

Yes, it is.

In fact, it's far worse here on the ground because all the ugliness you can see from thousands of miles away, outside of a few politicians' faces, is probably still rather abstract: a largely undefinable, faceless wave of malice and bigotry; something to be analyzed and studied later.

But here on the ground, this malignant sickness has taken over the faces of far too many...faces that have now become far too familiar:

They are the faces of family members whose newly revealed racism is regularly leveling us around the dinner table.

They are the faces of former church friends who have completely abandoned the Jesus they claim faith in, and in his place have chosen the vilest of idols.

They are the faces of once pleasant neighbors who casually regurgitate extremist propaganda in sidewalk conversations.

They are the faces of childhood friends spewing anti-immigrant filth on their social media profiles and posts.

They are the faces of store owners and hair stylists and restaurant workers, whose interactions with us have now become walks through minefields.

So, yes, it's the staggering cruelty of those holding the power here—*and, just as much*, it's the people we know and live alongside who are so gladly empowering them.

Yes, it's the complete bastardization of the rule of law and the systems of protections our forebears put in place to avoid putting our nation in such peril—*and* it's our coworkers and uncles and classmates who don't seem to give a damn about that.

Yes, it's our president's absolute sociopathic lack of empathy and his unrepentant viciousness—*and* it's the people we've shared Thanksgiving dinner with and served on mission trips alongside who share his venom and boost his signal.

Yes, it's our government's incessant attacks on LGBTQ people and immigrants and Muslims and the sick and the vulnerable—*and* it's the once kind-hearted people we love, who have been so poisoned by partisan talking points and perverted Christian theology that they celebrate all of it.

*That's why this is all so bad.*

We're certainly losing the big things here: the integrity of our elections, the stability of our republic, the faith in our systems, the illusion that our Republican leaders will put anything over power and party.

*And we're losing much more than that.*

We're losing the soft places we called home: our families and our churches and our circle of friends.

We are swiftly and almost hourly seeing the relational fractures that may have always been there beneath the surface, and that are now visible and cavernous.

We're trying to decide whether to fight for relationships we've spent our lives nurturing, or whether we need to sever those connections in the name of self-preservation.

These things will never make the news or make a global impact—but they are shattering our personal worlds down to their bedrock.

So we're marching and protesting and working and resisting in the face of this monumental and historically malevolent national political cancer—and while we're doing that, we're also trying to preserve our families and our friendships and our workplaces, which are all so often hanging by a thread these days.

This is a constitutional crisis and it's a family emergency.

We're wondering what happened to our nation—and what the hell happened to our grandparents, siblings, and best friends.

Yes, American Democracy is in peril, *and* our most treasured relationships with people are in tatters, too.

We are trying to salvage both—and it's exhausting.

So yes, friends around the world, thank you for caring about us in America.

It *is* as bad as it looks from where you're standing.

*And* it's far worse, too.

# CHAPTER TWENTY ONE

# Colin Kaepernick Was Right About Us

Colin Kaepernick was right about us, white America.

He was right to kneel because when he did, he fully exposed us.

He exposed us as we became viscerally disgusted—not by the reckless disregard of black lives, but by the earnest and open declaration of black grief at their premature passing.

He exposed us when we felt it was our right to tell another human being how to express *their* personal freedoms, during an anthem supposedly devoted to celebrating those personal freedoms.

He exposed us when we treasured flags and songs over flesh and blood; when we repeatedly ignored dissenting facts in order to hold onto our easy and lazy outrage.

He exposed us when we chose to listen to the words of a divisive white president over athletes of color as to their motives and intentions.

He exposed us as we had the stratospheric nerve to lecture him about the right way for him to protest as a citizen of this country.

He exposed us when we chastised him for the manner in which he expressed his freedom, because it was a little too "free" for us.

He exposed us as we saw all these things—and still remained silent.

And he's exposing us now—those of us who are burning shoes and cutting up socks and boycotting Nike because a strong man of color who will not be shamed into silence or allow us to make the rules still makes our blood boil—the most telling and tragic truth of all.

Privilege is a terrible disease because it is invisible to those most fully afflicted with it. When most deeply in the throes of this heart sickness, they cannot see themselves or the reality of the moment.

They do not require data to be disgusted or truth to craft the narrative of their suffering. They simply feel fear, even when it is unfounded; oppression, even when there is none; offensiveness, even when they have no cause.

If you're seething right now, this is a symptom.

If you're still doubling down on some imagined defense of "America" while simultaneously seeking to deny people of color America's most elemental liberties, you're proving Colin Kaepernick right.

If you're still refusing to believe the players' voices over the one in your head or in a president's tweets or in an angry country singer's rants, you're showing why Kaepernick was correct to protest from the very beginning.

You're confirming the very reason his knee first hit the turf two years ago: Too many white people want to go through life undisturbed by any reality of their advantages.

They will do anything not to be inconvenienced by the ugly realities in a system of which they are the greatest beneficiaries.

They will be profoundly pissed off when a person of color intrudes on their entertainment with a dose of sobering truth about life and death.

They will follow the most convoluted, nonsensical thought lines if this allows them to quiet marginalized people and evade culpability for their own prejudices toward those marginalized people.

It isn't surprising that the folks so violently shaken by Colin Kaepernick profess to defend a freedom they don't like him exercising.

They're the same ones saying that they love America—and a draft-dodging, Russian-beholden, POW-belittling president.

They're the same people who say they want to rewind and reclaim America's "greatness" while ignoring how much suffering and injustice that supposed greatness created for so many.

They're the same people who claim allegiance to both Jesus and to Donald Trump.

Cognitive dissonance doesn't register when you're white and terrified of losing your dominance.

By kneeling, Colin Kaepernick let us do the work for him.

He didn't need to belabor the point; he just let us show ourselves.

He allowed white America's responses to reveal who we are.

He saw something ugly in us that we didn't and still don't want to see.

And he was right.

CHAPTER TWENTY TWO

# The Christian Right Was Right

I confess that I was dead wrong about this. I have to hand it to the Christian Right; they knew what the heck they were talking about all this time. They knew this was going to happen and predicted it with astounding accuracy, over and over again.

For decades they tried to tell us that the sky was falling, that devils were walking among us, that the end was so very nigh. For years and years, they lamented the approaching devastation and tried to prepare us like good prophets do. They pounded their pulpits with ferocity and thumped their Bibles with abandon, forecasting this country's certain doom—and we didn't listen. We rolled our eyes and dismissed them as out-of-touch, hypocritical, religious zealots whose hold on reality was tenuous at best. And yet, they had it right all along.

It turns out that every single one of their raw-throated, brimstone-breathing prophecies were true:

That the wolves would come in sheep's clothing to devour the innocent.
That there would be a twisting of the Scriptures to justify vile evil of every kind.
That people would do what was right in their own eyes and make themselves into the very God they most worshiped.
That money and power and pride would be too seductive to avoid for far too many.
That the Church was in danger of being polluted to the point of death.
That the least of these would be discarded and brutalized.
That good people would be preyed upon by opportunistic monsters.

These sage prognosticators had *everything* about the approaching disaster correct—except its source.
They neglected to predict the actual genesis of this great decimation. Because it wouldn't be the Gays or the Muslims or the Atheists or celebrities or street people or tattooed women or sexually active teenagers, as they'd so foretold. It wouldn't be transgender people lurking in bathrooms, or brown-skinned suicide bombers from some distant cave, or any of the countless boogeymen they told us were hiding in the shadows to bring terror. No, the encroaching danger was a whole lot closer than all that.

For years, the Christian Right has been warning us about godless hordes coming to destroy America, and it turns out this was true—it's just that the words were autobiographical.

As a lifelong Christian, I've had a sick sense of déjà vu watching politicians professing to be followers of Jesus dismantling every program designed to care for the vulnerable and the hurting; seeing the way the powerful are being awarded greater power; watching empathy vanishing and hatred skyrocketing. I've heard this story a million times before: proclaimed on Sunday mornings from pulpits, unleashed in religious social media rants, and shouted through bullhorns on street corners. I knew this was coming, or at least I should have. We all should have. These harbingers of doom were absolutely right to warn us—and ironically they were the very ones they were warning us about. In the sickest kind of self-fulfilling prophecy, they were the plague of these days that they said would come.

It would be the preachers and the evangelists abandoning the heart of Jesus, perverting the words of the Bible for their agenda, selling their souls for a high place overlooking the world. They would be the very false prophets they told us that we should run like hell from. These supposed disciples of Jesus would be the ones to betray him with a kiss and send him to a bloody, undignified end.

Yes, the Christian Right was right; evil was going to run amok through the world and terrorize the lives of ordinary people and make a mockery of God. And that is what it is surely doing these days.

I owe them an apology.

I should have believed them.

I once was blind, and now I see.

CHAPTER TWENTY THREE

# The Cult of Trump

"I don't recognize her anymore."

Through choked-back tears, a man shared these words today about his 74-year old mother. The last two years have seen their once-loving relationship deteriorate precipitously. It's now relegated to cold exchanges via text and strained small talk at family gatherings, sandwiched between explosive screaming matches which are often followed by extended periods of radio silence.

He shared screenshots of his mother's Facebook profile, littered with Alt-Right talking points, discriminatory memes, and effusive tributes to the president—always juxtaposed with hateful diatribes regarding our former president. The racism and homophobia and Islamophobia she generates every day is both shocking and devastating to her adult son.

"She just believes every word out of his mouth, everything she watches on Fox News." he said. "I can't reason with her. It's like talking to someone who's been brainwashed. She isn't the mother I grew up with."

This is how cults work: They gradually alter people's brains, attuning them to a singular voice, and weaponizing them against any dissenting opinions. To their manipulated minds, efforts to reach them with objective truth become acts of aggression against the one they see as divine—and trigger an ever-more passionate affection toward their leader. They will defend that one person even to the relational deaths with others they once loved.

America is in a cultic crisis, and Trumpism is the cult. There is no other way to approach these days.

When you believe one man above Science, above our intelligence agencies, above former CIA directors and retired generals and revered journalists—when you believe that one man above even your own eyes and ears—you are fully indoctrinated.

This hasn't happened by accident, but by sickening design. Cult leaders prey upon emotionally vulnerable people— leveraging their loneliness, their disenfranchisement, their disconnection. They bombard their targets with a steady stream of misinformation, incendiary rhetoric, and chaotic prophecy— and into the swirling confusion created inside their targets' heads, they come promising safety and security, while having no concern for their cult members at all. They start a fire—and rush in with a bucket of water.

Donald Trump has mastered the art of emergency manufacturing and danger generation. We saw this during the near month-long government shutdown. He convinced his followers that violent, drug-carrying immigrants were streaming across the border to duct tape and rape women; he then feigned courage by boldly and publicly vowing to protect them by shutting down the government. He then did so and, after weeks of complete inactivity and not a single change, stood in the White House Rose Garden claiming victory against a fictional adversary by stopping an unnecessary crisis that he alone created.

Every day he designs a false threat, steps onto the nonexistent battlefield, and declares himself victorious to a group of now emotionally dependent human beings whose internal stories and well-being depends on him winning. That's the only way their world makes sense anymore; it is the only outcome they can conceive of.

People who've tried to rescue their loved ones from such inculcation will tell you how incredibly difficult it is to deprogram them after such repeated deception, such prolonged lying, such protracted fear. They will detail the excruciating efforts to reach parents and best friends and adult children through the haze of their addiction to the connection they have come to feel with someone who is predatory toward them. And many will describe the long and bloody battles they've fought for the people they love—battles they sometimes ultimately lost to the cult.

My friend said of his mother, "I'm going to keep trying to reach her because I know who she used to be. I'm still hopeful I can get her back."

This needs to be the posture we choose now. No one willingly joins a cult. They are lured and tricked and coerced all the way up to the precipice of emotional and intellectual surrender— and then they fall in. Once there, it is nearly impossible for them to leave voluntarily. They can't see that they are fighting against their own self-interest by aligning with the one holding them hostage.

Leaving isn't an option, so someone who loves them persistently and fiercely needs to brave the wounding words and the violent opposition to try rescuing them.

The only way they can do that is by loving them in a way that the cult leader simply isn't capable of—and by refusing to let his voice be the only voice left that they hear.

# CHAPTER TWENTY FOUR

# No, White MAGA Friend—You Weren't "Embarrassed" by Barack Obama

I remember the day after the 2016 Presidential Election, a friend of mine who happens to be white remarked on social media that he "finally wasn't embarrassed of America and our President."

I sprained my eyes rolling them and they have never fully recovered.

Since then, I've heard this sentiment echoed by more white folks than I can count, especially in recent months...supposed relief at once again having a leader who instills pride.

Since I don't have the time to ask each of them individually, I'll ask here:

So, you were embarrassed for the past 8 years, huh?

Really?

What *exactly* were you embarrassed by?

Were you embarrassed by his one and enduring twenty-five year marriage to a strong woman he's never ceased to publicly praise, respect, or cherish?

Were you embarrassed by the way he lovingly and sweetly parented and protected his daughters?

Were you embarrassed by his Columbia University degree in Political Science or his graduating magna cum laude from Harvard Law School?

Maybe you were embarrassed by his white American and Black Kenyan parents, or by the diversity he was raised in viewed as normal or as welcomed news?

Were you embarrassed by his eloquence, his quick wit, his easy humor, his seeming comfort meeting with both world leaders and street cleaners; by his bright smile or his sense of empathy or his steadiness—perhaps by his lack of personal scandals or verbal gaffes or impulsive tirades?

No. Of course you weren't.

Honestly, I don't believe you were ever embarrassed. That word implies an association that brings ridicule, one that makes you ashamed by association, and if *that's* something you claim to have experienced over the past eight years by having Barack Obama representing you in the world—I'm going to suggest you rethink your word choice.

You weren't "embarrassed" by Barack Obama.

You were threatened by him.
You were intimidated by him.
You were challenged by him.
You were triggered by him.

But I don't believe it had anything to do with his resume or his experience or his character or his conduct in office—because you seem fully proud right now to be associated with a three-time married, serial adulterer and confessed predator; a man whose election and business dealings and relationships are riddled with controversy and malfeasance. You're perfectly fine being represented by a bullying, vile, obnoxious, genitalia-grabbing, Tweet-ranting, prime minister-shoving charlatan who's managed to offend all our allies and alienate millions of our citizens in a few short months. And you're okay with him putting on religious faith like a rented, dusty, ill-fitting tuxedo and immediately tossing it in the garbage when he's finished with it.

None of that you're embarrassed by? I wonder how that works.

Actually, I'm afraid I have an idea.

Listen, you're perfectly within your rights to have disagreed with Barack Obama's policies or to have taken issue with his tactics. No one's claiming he was a flawless politician or a perfect human being. But somehow I don't think that's what we're talking about here. I think the thing President Obama did that *really* upset you, white friend—was having a complexion that was far darker than you were ever comfortable with. I think the president we have now feels much better, even at his orangest.

Because objectively speaking, if what's happening in our country right now doesn't cause you great shame and doesn't induce the continual meeting of your palm to your face—I don't believe embarrassment is ever something you struggle with.

No, if you claimed to be embarrassed by Barack Obama but you're somehow not embarrassed by Donald Trump—I'm going to strongly suggest it was largely a pigmentation issue.

And as an American and a Christian committed to diversity and equality and to the liberty at the heart of this nation—*that* embarrasses me.

# CHAPTER TWENTY FIVE

# No, Christian, Jesus Didn't Say You Can Have Your Guns

In the wake of the shameful growing legacy of mass shootings in America, one of the saddest realizations is that the loudest, most vehement voices championing the cause of weapons of brutality have come from professed Evangelical Christians.

The cognitive dissonance of supposed *followers of Jesus* choosing the side of violence and opposing the movement of mercy is staggering, and exceeded only by the contention that Jesus says they can pack heat.

It's nonsense and heresy and it's a full bastardization of his life and ministry.

There simply aren't any theological gymnastics wild enough to make it work.

Not with the Jesus who preached that those following in his footsteps would turn the other cheek to violence.

Not with the Jesus who spoke of the blessed nature of the peacemakers.

Not with the Jesus whose benevolence and lack of force were ever-present.

Gun-loving Jesus followers fondly point to a passage in the Gospel biography written by Luke, where Jesus speaks about his impending unlawful arrest by Roman soldiers and instructs them to "bring a sword."

This, they claim, is their God-given gun license.

The problem is that they stop reading at this point, close the book—and run to their gun shows and NRA rallies.

They fail to stick with the same story for a couple more paragraphs, when the Romans arrive and one of Jesus' students named Peter takes out one of the swords, and cuts off a soldier's ear. Jesus verbally tears into Peter, heals the soldier's ear, and tells those with him that this will not be their way.

He then allows himself to be taken into custody, beaten, and ultimately murdered by his captors.

This is the full story, and it is bad news for those wanting to be cowboys.

This narrative isn't helpful for the gun-toting followers of Jesus.
This narrative doesn't give them a God who consents to their
weapon lust.
This narrative doesn't let them have Jesus and NRA membership
at the same time.
This narrative actually tells them to drop their weapons and beat
them into plowshares and to be those who live differently than
the fear-bringers.

Christians straining to hold on to their guns talk about the story
of Jesus fashioning a whip to drive moneylenders out of the
temple as some half-baked gun blessing—which, again, is such
a perversion of the story that it would be laughable if it weren't
resulting in so many dead school students two thousand
years later.

Jesus chases the corrupt people out of the temple *because they
are profiting from the manipulation of religion.* Jesus is driving
out the modern-day NRA lobbyists, corrupt politicians, and
religious hypocrites. He is running the vipers off—and they are
the vipers. And, by the way, he doesn't strike or kill any of them
in the process.

This is why people outside of Christianity think that followers
of Jesus picking up the cause of tools of mass murder and rapid
carnage is a blasphemous disconnect—because it is.
They're seeing it all perfectly clearly.
They can see people trying desperately to make God in their
own fearful, insecure, bullying image—and reject it all.
They know enough about Jesus to know that his finger
would never be on a trigger—and there's simply no way
to get around that.

In a last-gasp attempt to hold Jesus at gunpoint, these folks love to quote him talking in Matthew's Gospel about his mission "not to bring peace, but a sword."

Again, they desperately want *those words*, but not their context or their intention. Jesus is speaking about the way his teachings will cause turbulence between people; the way interpersonal conflict will arrive when they endeavor to do his work of love, compassion, and justice: It will drive a wedge, it will cause a rift—it will bring a sword. He isn't saying he wants us to lay waste to our family members. He isn't saying he came to bring people to hand-to-hand combat. (Yes, gun advocate Christians actually try to go here, to this ridiculous place.)

Those professing to take such words literally must also be prepared to gouge their eyes out for looking at a woman lustfully—though I imagine this would leave a vast army of blind faithful folks in churches this coming Sunday.

No, Christian, Jesus wants no part of your gun lust. He wants nothing to do with your seething nationalism and your 2nd Amendment shield and your tough guy bravado behind a trigger.

He told you to love your enemies.
He told you to turn your cheek.
He told you to resist an evil person.
He told you to be foot washers and wound binders and compassion givers.
He told you to care for the least and to feed the poor and to welcome the refugee.
*That* is what he said clearly.

You can love your guns.

You can open carry in department stores.

You can champion the cause of assault weapons.

You can cover your bumper in tough guy propaganda.

You can oppose any sensible gun regulations.

You can glory in your amassed arsenal.

You can do nothing while thousands of people die every year in America.

Just don't try to pretend Jesus is okay with it.

He isn't.

He weeps at it all.

And so do those of us who understand.

# CHAPTER TWENTY SIX

# The Privilege of Positivity

Yesterday a friend on social media challenged me to "only post positive messages for one whole day."

It felt like part social media campaign, part enthusiastic dare, and part gentle personal scolding.

I hear a similar sentiment by many people in a myriad of ways, expressing the same concern to people around them: *you're producing too much negativity here*.

Most people mean well and, believe me, I do understand the sentiment—but honestly I don't know what "positive" means to some people anymore. It seems like something is being lost in translation.

To many people, *positive* means to only speak happy words, to only focus on pleasant things, to never be combative or angry or grieving, to say nothing critical or confrontational to or about anyone.

It means pictures of babies and puppies and happy people on vacation—not of families in cages or deplorable detention centers or dying wildlife.

It means videos of cats in funny clothes—not of young unarmed black men being beaten by police during "routine" traffic stops.

It means beaming-smile selfies and feel good platitudes and perfectly framed food porn.

The request to "be positive" seems to mean please avoid giving someone any information (or providing that information in a way) that derails the path and plans and emotional state of their day. If it causes another person to become angry or to grieve or if it rubs up against a set of assumptions they have—then it's negative.

We all have a natural empathy saturation point: a threshold we reach where the bad news is too much to absorb. With so much to be burdened by these days, the desire to escape some of it is natural and understandable—but it's also a sure sign of our privilege that we think we can.

The very idea that we can have the option of escaping terrible news or sidestepping difficult conversations or limiting disturbing information is itself confirmation that we are buffered from a good deal of struggle. That we can tire of a story or an issue likely means we have no real personal stake in it.

Many people don't have the option of avoiding negativity today.
They don't have the privilege of not coming off as combative.
They don't have the luxury of *not* fighting.
They can't decide not to live with urgency on this day, because
there is no other way to live in order to survive it.

There aren't a lot of migrants or Muslims or people without
healthcare or survivors of sexual assault or parents of
transgender teens saying, "Can you give me more puppy videos
and less truthful news about how broken our nation is?"

To me, *activism* is pure positivity.

It is passionately affirming humanity by taking note of the places
it is most endangered and assailed.

It's being *for someone* enough to advocate for them when they
are vulnerable and marginalized and invisible.

Being positive means being fully engaged in real life.

I'm all for looking for the good in people, for leaning into the
hope, for staying optimistic about the future, for boosting
encouragement, for cultivating joy, for taking the time to enjoy
meaningful moments with people you love...even sharing puppy
photos. But that has nothing to do with editing what I share
so that it feels more pleasant or palatable to people who are
shielded from danger enough to be annoyed by its news.

Yes, please give people funny videos and heartwarming images
and stuff to make them laugh and breathe and rest. The world
needs these things.

But as often as we share beautifully crafted Instagram images, we need to make sure we're showing people reality completely unfiltered as well. The world needs this, too.

If being positive means not calling out abject racism,
if it means not advocating for migrant families in cages,
if it means silently ignoring human rights atrocities,
if it means allowing my LGBTQ friends to have their
rights eroded,
if it means making peace with bigotry in the highest levels of our government,
if it means abiding Muslims being vilified,
if it means allowing legislative violence to go unopposed,
if it means standing by fellow white Christians who pervert the message of Jesus,
if it means avoiding unpleasant conversations about the things that burden my heart because they make other people uncomfortable...

Then I guess I won't be positive today.

Actually, I'm positive about that.

# CHAPTER TWENTY SEVEN

# Lessons Trump Supporters Are Teaching Their Children

*Teach your children well. Their father's hell did slowly go by. And feed them on your dreams. The one they pick's the one you'll know by.*—Crosby, Stills, Nash, and Young

One thing you learn as you raise children is that they're always watching, always listening, always learning—that you are always teaching them something: your values, how to treat people, how to be a human being.

I wonder if people supporting this president and this administration realize what they're teaching their children; what boosting his tweets and applauding his rally rants and celebrating his legislative assaults on vulnerable people are telling them.

Whether they realize it or not, they're teaching their children…

*People don't matter.* Human beings are things wielded in battles you manufacture in order to win. The actual flesh and blood lives on the other side of your stereotypes and slurs and caricatures? They have no intrinsic value. The moment you can dehumanize a person you've never met is the moment you free yourself from any responsibility for the damage you do or applaud someone else doing to them.

*Never apologize.* When you are found to be wrong or speak in error—never admit it. No matter how far afield of facts you find yourself or how grievous the mistake or how divorced of reality your initial statements may have been—simply double down, gaslight people, and attack your critic's credibility and integrity. But never admit the error and never, under any circumstance, apologize. That is failure.

*Diversity is dangerous.* The more differences around you, the more there is to fear. Threats always come from those who aren't like you. If someone's pigmentation or orientation or nation of origin don't match your own, they're probably someone you want to avoid or be wary of. Never seek out difference. Exclusion and self-preservation are the best defenses against the evils in the world.

*It's all about you.* Forget the advice of your teachers and pastors and story books, and discard all that nonsense about loving your neighbor as yourself or doing unto others as you'd have done to you. Other people's experiences are unimportant. In this Universe, you are the solitary sun around which every other body revolves. The more you allow other people to be seen and heard, the less you will be able to thrive. This is a zero-sum game and there is only one winner.

*Compassion is a flaw.* To feel empathy is to show weakness. Sitting with people long enough to see them and understand their story and to feel a bit of their pain will only slow you down. The more callous you can become, the less vulnerable you are. The greatest virtue in this life is simply not to give a damn about other people. A dead heart is much better than a bleeding one.

*America is the world.* Some people will tell you that all human beings on the planet have value, that humanity is one interdependent community sharing the same home, that a child five thousand miles away is as important as one down the street or the one in your nursery. Don't buy it. The place where you live and the people who live there are better than everyone else.

*Women are less valuable than men.* Consent is irrelevant. Autonomy is a myth. A woman's body does not belong to her. She exists solely for the pleasure and purpose of men, and this is true of wives and partners and blind dates and people you pass on the street. Whatever you do to women, no matter how vile, you will never be made accountable for.

*Cheat to win.* The desired ends justify any possible means, no matter how vile or despicable. Rig every system, fix every game, stack every deck—and justify it all because the victory is all that matters. Fair play and honesty and being a person of honor are all of little value. What really matters is the prize, so be sure to get it. Winning is worth both someone else's pain and your soul.

*Whiteness is better.* You'll hear a lot about equality and you'll even pretend it matters to you, but don't believe it for a second. God may have made all people in his image, but Caucasians bear far more resemblance. Never mind that if Adam and Eve existed, they came from a place without a Cracker Barrel; just know that your pigmentation makes you superior to the "bad people" and those from "shithole countries."

*Your convictions are for sale.* Everything has a price—your word, your allegiance, your vote...even your soul. Don't waste any time trying to cultivate personal morality or forming a code of ethics or standing for anything. Those things will only weigh you down and hinder your success. Instead, find which way the wind is blowing and move that way. See who the likely winners will be and cast your lots with them. Don't worry about your soul—take the cash.

*Laws don't apply to you.* In theory, society has rules and they must be followed by everyone (well, not you, of course). It will be important to give lip service to "doing things the right way" and to "valuing the Constitution" and to "obeying the laws in place"—as such declarations will divert people's attention from you disregarding anything that prevents your advancement or profiteering. But find the loopholes and use them; that's why they're there.

*Religion is a prop.* Faith is simply a costume to put on when it profits you...a shiny veneer to cover yourself in, in order to ingratiate yourself into community with genuinely spiritual people who will think the best of you, and thus will be easily fooled. Wield religious values like a rented tuxedo: Wear them in public for special events and soon discard them.

*When in doubt, lie.* The truth is malleable. It is something fluid. You get to define it for yourself and for those who listen to you. Have no concern about facts or objective reality or data; instead, over and over and over, speak untruth with conviction. Tell the lies with confidence and suddenly they will become true.

A generation of children is learning these things from the people most entrusted to show them how to be human. These people are molding the lenses the children see the world through from birth. It will almost be impossible for them to discern reality.

The rest of us will have to do all we can to remind them that this simply isn't good or right or decent. The rest of us will have to do all we can to help them transcend their parents' prejudices and preferences—and to embrace interdependence and equality and compassion.

The world we become depends on it.

As a wise woman once said, "It takes a village."

# CHAPTER TWENTY EIGHT

# The One Sin White Evangelicals Couldn't Forgive Barack Obama For

Over eighty percent of white evangelicals—many of them women—voted for Donald Trump in 2016, less than two weeks after video surfaced of him speaking with historic vulgarity about women.

This started a pattern that would be repeated countless times in subsequent months, right up to the present second: professed Christians suddenly becoming "forgiving" because they had no other choice—supposed followers of Jesus whose choice to align with a devil simply could not be admitted under any circumstance.

Indeed, the 2016 election ushered in a new age of staggering miracles. We have seen, in white evangelicals and Donald Trump, a level of mercy they were simply incapable of during the previous eight years.

Yes, he said he could grab women by the pussy.
Yes, he said he "moved" on a married woman "like a bitch."
Yes, he said that he "tried to f*ck her."
Yes, he'd been credibly accused by multiple women of sexual assault.
Yes, he'd been an unapologetic serial adulterer.

A presidential candidate representing the Christian "Family Values" Party with this growing resume of immorality...Certainly, this abject ugliness would have been a spiritual disqualifier for men and women who were morally offended by President Obama in a tan suit? For a people fully outraged at Michelle Obama's bare upper arms? For believers indignant at the phrase "Happy Holidays" on a coffee cup? For Christians apparently sickened by the then president's supposed brilliantly-hidden Muslim faith?

Surely, Trump's putrid moral malfeasance would be a deal breaker for faithful disciples of Jesus.

Nope.

"He was a baby Christian."
"All men talk like that."
"He's repentant."

STUFF THAT NEEDS TO BE SAID

"He's forgiven by God."
"He's a changed man."

These would now be their default sermons...in response to the nearly hourly stomach-turning offenses and revelations that have followed: in the wake of every white supremacist cabinet appointment; every newly unearthed sign of election fraud; every dangerous social media attack on a war hero or civil rights trailblazer or Muslim political critic; every racially-charged rally diatribe; and every legislative attack on migrants.

And when Trump's actions were so sickening, his words so incendiary, his instability so obvious that such words of defense proved laughable—they summoned yet one more miracle from the heavens in his defense:

"God is using Donald Trump the way he used other sinners in the Bible."

So now the racial slurs and sexual assaults and extramarital affairs and "shithole country" contempt and Pocahontas nicknames and caged migrant children—instead of being clear evidence of his personal malignancy and lack of moral conviction of any kind—could be confirmation of his divine anointing.

The Lord really does work in mysterious ways.

As the moral filth has continued to flow from Donald Trump like sludge from a broken sewer pipe—over and over his white evangelical faithful have again and again found religion and embraced him anew, like a manure-covered prodigal son. They have quite spectacularly and repeatedly wiped away every brutal transgression in a way that would have been impossible in the eight years before 2016. What a miraculous movement of the Spirit we're seeing in these followers of Jesus, that the exposed breasts of this First Lady are suddenly less offensive than the bared shoulders of another; that a First Daughter invading our political process is less concerning than one drinking wine; that Donald Trump is placed here by God and worthy of evangelical support, but Obama was installed by the devil and deserving of damnation.

Maybe it's God—or maybe it's the fact that Barack Obama simply committed the one sin that these proclaimed lovers of God were never going to be able to forgive. For all his grievous transgressions, there was one that Donald Trump was never going to be able to commit even if he wanted to.

Many white evangelicals have forgiven Donald Trump for multiple affairs, porn star payoffs, financial improprieties, unhinged Twitter rants, Russian alliances, and vile moral filth of every kind—despite him never asking for it or repenting in any way.

Yet they've never forgiven Barack Obama for being black.

It was his original sin.

It turns out that was something they simply could never abide.

To them his pigmentation was and is an abomination—and even a dark-skinned Jewish Jesus born in the Middle East couldn't help them find that kind of mercy.

# CHAPTER TWENTY NINE

# Letter to an American Gun Lover

If you're an American gun lover, I'm not going to argue with you today.

I'm not going to exchange news articles and opinion pieces and stat graphics.

I'm not going to absorb lazy, tired platitudes about people *killing people* or about *heart problems*.

I'm not going to respond to personal attacks or allegations of my disregard for your individual freedoms.

I'm not going to debate which acts of terrorism are worth decrying and which are worth justifying.

I'm not going to compare body counts and skin colors and shooters' names.

I'm not going to trade snarky insults or angry tirades or verbal jousts.

I'm not going to play one religion against another in ascribing culpability.

I'm not going to listen to critiques that I've become "too political" over something that, to me, is far greater than politics.

I'm not going to engage in violence with you as a way of protesting violence.

I *am* going to spend today trying to create a more peaceful world in whatever way that I can.

I am going to spend it practicing the compassion and benevolence and kindness that I preach, as much as I am able.

I am going to spend it fully grieving the loss of *all* innocent life.

I am going to spend it lamenting the fact that no amount of bloodshed seems to merit any action from you other than fiercely holding on to the horrible status quo.

I am going to spend it mourning the fact that Sandy Hook wasn't enough, that Charleston wasn't, that Colorado Springs wasn't, that Orlando wasn't, that Parkland wasn't enough—to move you.

I am going to spend it grieving those who devalue life—and those who do nothing when it is squandered.

I am going to spend it knowing that, for as long as I live, I will always represent one less gun in the world.

I am going to spend it trusting that a "bleeding heart" is always better than a dead one.

I am going to spend it being a person of *life*, surrounded by so much unnecessary death.

I am going to spend it living out my personal faith convictions that tell me I cannot repay evil for evil; that I must turn the other cheek; that I must pray for my enemies; that I don't get to take an eye for an eye.

And I am going to do it all armed solely with the belief that Love is the only weapon worthy of stockpiling and advocation.

I will not engage in *another* shootout today.

I will lay down my guns.

I will not return fire.

Peace.

# CHAPTER THIRTY

# Pick a Hill Worth Dying On, America

If your eyes are clear and open right now, you can see it: This is a pivot point for us, America.

It is the place where we collectively turn back toward our best selves or slide into the abyss of the very worst of us. We are, in real-time, crafting our shared legacy—and the world is watching to see who we will be. Our children are watching, too.

These are historic days and they will be recorded; they will tell the story of this country, as either the time good people crossed lines of political party, faith tradition, and racial divide, and course corrected us out of abject disaster—or the days we all stopped giving a damn and fully consented to the darkness for good. These will be marked as the moments we succumbed to a thousand small assaults on decency—or when we decided to stop the bleeding altogether.

There is no question anymore for those not deluded by supremacy or religion or self-preservation: This thing currently steering us is an abomination.

It is an abandonment of empathy, a rejection of personal liberty, human rights violations, a squandering of radiant lives.
There is nothing redemptive or life-giving in it.
The only question remaining is if you're okay with it, and you get to answer for yourself—by your movement or your inaction.

In these very seconds, you and I get to decide whether our children and grandchildren will inherit something beautiful or something grotesque. It's really that simple, that elemental—that close.

This is not about waiting for God or a political party or a social media celebrity to do something, or for some faceless people you imagine will rescue you.

No, friend, there is no superhero flying in to save the day—you need to save it.

And the way you will save it is by finding whatever it is that pulls you out of the paralyzing funk of grief and sadness and disbelief you've been in—and into the jagged trenches of passionate resistance.

You save it by deciding what matters most in this life, and whether it matters enough to do more than you're doing to defend and protect it right now. In the presence of such great hatred, you are either an activist or an accomplice; the vocal opposition or a willing partner.

You and I need to pick a hill worth dying on right now, and we need to ascend it without delay. We need to speak and write and work and protest and vote, and do all the things we've been waiting for someone else to do.

This movement may cause friction in our families.
It may bring turbulence to our marriages.
It may yield collateral damage to our careers.
It may cost us financially and personally.
It may alienate us from our neighbors.
It may push us from our churches.
It may be inconvenient and uncomfortable and painful—but that is the price of liberty, and you and I need to pay it because other people paid it before us.
No excuses will be good enough to the generations that follow us about why we did nothing, so we need to stop trying to find them.

I don't know what matters enough to move you from complacency or indecision or selfishness or apathy:
the atrocities dealt to so many humans,
the perversions of Christianity,
the pillaging of the environment,
the violations of our Constitution,
the cries of migrant children,
the hijacking of the Supreme Court,
the dismantling of healthcare,
the long-ignored school shootings,
the harassment of LGBTQ teens,

the assaults on women's autonomy over their bodies,
the malice of our public servants,
the twisting of truth,
the marching of Nazis in our streets,
the dumbing down of our discourse.

Is it love or equality or compassion or diversity or humanity?

I don't know what is worth *you* doing something right now—
but *you* do.

So instead of lamenting how horrible it all is—accept the
invitation to make it less horrible.
Instead of looking to the sky and wondering why no one is doing
anything—you do something.
Step out of the cloistered place of your private despair, and into a
jacked-up world that you can alter by showing up.
Use your gifts and your influence and your breath and your
hands—and fix something that is badly broken before it breaks
beyond repair.

This is not some fictional zombie apocalypse series you can
binge watch, turn off, and walk away from into the radiant
light of day. This is flesh and blood men and women living
among you, with dangerous agendas they will not abandon
unless opposed.

I'm not trying to scare you. What is happening right now in this
nation should scare you enough. I'm trying to wake you up and
ask you to see if your heart is still beating. If you can say yes,
then do something worthy of that gift.

Whatever hill is worth dying on for you in this life, *take it now*.

Affirm life, speak truth, defend the vulnerable, call out injustices—and gladly brave the criticisms and the wounds you will sustain in doing it, knowing that they are a small price to pay for the nation that *could be* if you speak—or the nation that *will be* if you do not.

Chances are you won't actually be called to die for these causes and these people, but when you do leave this planet you will have lived for them. That, in itself, will be a beautiful legacy.

If you aren't finding your voice right now, don't bother worrying about it later.

You won't have one much longer.

Ascend the hill.

PART THREE

# Stuff That Needs To Be Said About Life, Death, Grief, and Depression

CHAPTER THIRTY ONE

# Everyone Around You Is Grieving. Go Easy.

The day I learned my father died, I went to the grocery store to buy bananas.

I remember thinking to myself, *This is insane. Your dad just died. Why the hell are you buying bananas?*

But we needed bananas. We'd be waking up for breakfast tomorrow morning, and there wouldn't be any bananas—so there I was.

And lots of other stuff still needed doing, too; so over the coming days I would navigate parking lots, wait in restaurant lines, and sit on park benches pushing back tears, fighting to stay upright, and—in general—always being seconds from a total, blubbering, room-clearing freak out.

I wanted to wear a sign that said: I JUST LOST MY DAD. PLEASE GO EASY.

Unless anyone passing by looked deeply into my bloodshot eyes or noticed the occasional break in my voice and thought enough to ask, it's not like they'd have known what was happening inside me or around me. They wouldn't have had any idea of the gaping sinkhole that had just opened up and swallowed the normal life of the guy next to them in the produce section.

And while I didn't want to physically wear my circumstances on my chest, it probably would have caused people around me to give me space or speak and move more carefully—and it might have made the impossible almost bearable.

Everyone around you—the people you share the grocery store line with, pass in traffic, sit next to at work, encounter on social media, and see across the kitchen table—they're all experiencing the collateral damage of living. They are all grieving someone, missing someone, worried about someone. Their marriages are crumbling or their mortgage payment is late or they're waiting on their child's test results or they're getting bananas five years after a death and still pushing back tears because the loss feels as real as it did that first day.

Every single human being you pass by today is fighting to find peace and to push back fear; to get through their daily tasks without breaking down in front of the bananas or in the carpool line or at the post office.

Maybe they aren't mourning the sudden, tragic passing of a parent, but wounded, exhausted, pain-ravaged people are everywhere everyday, stumbling all around us—and yet most of the time we're fairly oblivious to them:

*Parents whose children are terminally ill.*
*Couples in the middle of divorce.*
*People grieving the loss of loved ones and relationships.*
*Kids being bullied at school.*
*Teenagers who want to end their lives.*
*People marking the anniversary of a death.*
*Parents worried about their depressed teenager.*
*Spouses whose partners are deployed in combat.*
*Families with no idea how to keep the lights on.*
*Single parents with little help and little sleep.*

Everyone is grieving and worried and fearful, and yet none of them wear the signs, none of them have labels, and none of them come with written warnings reading I'M STRUGGLING. BE KIND TO ME.

And since they don't, it's up to you and me to look more closely and more deeply at everyone around us. Whether we're at work or at the gas station or in the produce section, we need to assume they are all just hanging by a thread, because most people are hanging by a thread—and our simple kindness can be that thread.

We need to remind ourselves just how hard the hidden stories around us might be, and approach each person as a delicate, breakable, invaluable treasure... and handle them with care.

As you make your way through the world today, people won't be wearing signs to announce their mourning or alert you to the attrition or broadcast how terrified they are—but if you look with the right eyes, you'll see the signs.

There are grieving people all around you.

Go easy.

CHAPTER THIRTY TWO

# When You Forget That They're Dead

Yesterday, I was sitting at my desk—head down and plowing through both the literal and figurative piles of tasks before me— when I took a quick pause to breathe and clear my head.

"I think I'll call dad," I thought to myself. Yet before the sentence had even reached its conclusion, everything stopped abruptly and I felt sick to my stomach.

"Damnit." I answered aloud and sighed heavily. Tears clouded my eyes until they spilled out onto the papers below me.

It had happened again.

My father's been dead for almost five years now, and this still happens more times than I care to admit. When I'm busy or stressed out or angry, that heart muscle memory kicks in and prompts me to reach for the phone—and then I remember.

For a millisecond, it's as if I forget that he's gone.

It sounds ridiculous that I could "not remember" this even for a millisecond...that I could possibly forget one of the people most dear to me isn't here any longer. But if you've ever lost someone you love, you understand.

You know the way grief sneaks up on you in the middle of an ordinary moment, when you least expect it to arrive—and it levels you.

You know that reflexive move to call them or hear their voice or to check in to see how their day is going...and what a kick in the gut you get when you remember you can't.

You know the fresh wave of grief that comes in the wake of the impossible "mistake" of your memory loss—and it's as if they're dying for the first time all over again.

As with all grieving, strangely, it's those excruciating moments that somehow console you, too. They hurt like hell, and then they comfort.

As painful as it is to be surprised by grief, it's a reminder of just how deeply connected your lives were, just how much a part of the rhythm of your days they had been, and just how beautiful it was to be loved by them for a million nondescript seconds in a million nondescript ways.

As you look back, it's those middle of the day phone calls, those surprise drop-in visits, those quick caresses to your hair, those seemingly meaningless conversations that become the most meaningful.

Maybe that's why you forget the people you love are gone. Maybe it's a gift to remind you of how it felt when they were here, when you were together, when nothing was out of reach.

I sat there at my desk crying, first in anger...then in gratitude. I had someone worth missing.

I know this is going to happen again and again. For as long as I live, whenever I have exciting news to share or when I'm frustrated or simply when I'm in the middle of an ordinary day, I know I'm going to forget and I'm going to reach for the phone.

I'll catch myself forgetting, and I'll wonder why it still happens.

Again I'll feel stupid, and tears will cloud my eyes.

And just like that, I'll remember how much I miss him.

And in a way that no words can measure, we'll be together again.

# CHAPTER THIRTY THREE

# Life Is Short. People Are Hurting. Don't Be a Jerk.

I walked around today and I looked at people; they were passing me in the grocery store, driving beside me on the highway, filling my news feed, walking by the house.

I tried to really see them.

I tried to look beneath the polished veneer they wore to imagine the invisible burdens they might be carrying beneath it: sick children, relational collapse, financial tension, crippling depression, profound grief, crisis of faith, loss of purpose—or maybe just the custom-designed multitude of the nagging insecurities and fears they've been carrying around since grade school and have never been able to shake.

As I looked at all these people, I wondered what kind of specific and personal hell they might be enduring, and it reminded me—so I'm reminding you:

Life is stunningly short and it is eggshell fragile.
Most people are having a really tough time.
They are almost always in more pain than you think they are.
Everyone is doing the very best they can to get through this day, and many are going through all manner of horrors in the process.
No one is immune from the invasive collateral damage of living.

And you don't have to save these people or fix them or give them any special treatment.

They are rarely asking for such things.

The thing these wounded and weary human beings need most from you as you share this space with them—is for you not be a jerk.

It's really that simple.

They need you *not to* contribute to their grieving, *not* to compound their sadness, *not* to amplify their fear, *not* to add to their adversity.

They need anything a little kinder than contempt from you.

They need you to embrace the vow of doctors and caregivers, of trying to *do no harm* to them.

This isn't difficult, either.

Actually, when it comes right down to it, *not being a jerk* is about as elementary as it gets:

Don't impose your religious beliefs on other people.
Don't demand that they adapt to your preferences of identity
or orientation.
Don't try to take away things that keep them physically healthy
or give them peace of mind or allow them access to education
or opportunity.
Don't put obstacles in a parent's way of caring for their children
or working to support them or guiding them safely into
adulthood.
Don't tell people who they can marry or how they should
worship or where they can call home.
Don't do things that make them more vulnerable to sickness
and sadness and stress.
Don't try to keep people from having things that you take for
granted.

Strangely enough, it's actually so much more work to be a jerk
to people—and yet so many seem hopelessly bent on it.

Right now in America, we are seeing what happens when people
discard the Golden Rule: when they abandon simple decency
and choose enmity, when they feel compelled to show cruelty
to strangers, when another's sorrow is of no concern.

On social media, in our school hallways, in our neighborhoods,
even in the highest levels of government, we are seeing an
epidemic of malevolence—men and women seemingly driven to
be hurtful and to do damage—human beings compelled to
be jerks.

Friends, I wish I could find a more eloquent, more poetic, less
abrasive way to say this—but I can't.

At the end of the day, so many of the grieving, struggling, fearful human beings filling up the landscape you find yourself in are hanging by the very thinnest of threads.

They are heroically pushing back despair, enduring real and imagined terrors, warring with their external circumstances and with their internal demons.

They are doing the very best they can, sometimes with little help or hope—and they just need those of us who live alongside them to make that *best-doing* a little easier.

These words are for me.
They're for you.
They're for ordinary people.
They're for our elected leaders.
They're for our president.
Life is short.
It is extremely fragile.
People are grieving.
They are struggling.
They are hurting.

For God's sake and for theirs—please just don't be a jerk.

CHAPTER THIRTY FOUR

# The Day I'll Finally Stop Grieving

"How long has it been? When is he going to get over that grief and move on already?"

I get it.

I know you might be thinking that about me or about someone else these days.

I know you may look at someone you know in mourning and wonder when they'll *snap out of it.*

I understand because I used to think that way, too.

Okay, maybe at the time I was self-aware enough or guilty enough not to think it quite that explicitly...even in my own head.

It might have come in the form of a growing impatience toward someone who was grieving or a gradual dismissing of their sadness over time or maybe in my intentionally avoiding them as the days passed. It was subtle, to be sure, but I can distinctly remember reaching the place where my compassion for grieving friends had reached its capacity—and it was long before they stopped hurting.

Like most people back then, I was operating under the faulty assumption that grief had some predictable expiration date: a reasonable period of time after which recovery and normalcy would come and the person would return to life as it was before, albeit with some minor adjustments.

I thought all these things—until I grieved.

I never think these things anymore.

Four years ago, I remember sitting with a dear friend at a coffee shop table in the aftermath of my father's sudden passing. In response to my quivering voice and my tear-weary eyes and my obvious shell shock, she assured me that this debilitating sadness—this ironic combination of searing pain and complete numbness—was going to give me a layer of compassion for hurting people that I'd never had before. It was an understanding, she said, that I simply couldn't have had without walking through the Grief Valley. She was right, though I would have gladly acquired this empathy in a million other ways.

Since that day, I've realized that Grief doesn't just visit you for a horrible, yet temporary holiday. It moves in, puts down roots—and it never leaves. Yes—as time passes, eventually the tidal waves subside for longer periods, but they inevitably come crashing in again without notice, when you are least prepared. With no warning, they devastate the landscape of your heart all over again, leaving you bruised and breathless and needing to rebuild once more.

Grief brings humility as a housewarming gift and doesn't care whether you want it or not.

You are forced to face your inability to do *anything* but feel it all and fall apart. It's incredibly difficult in those quiet moments, when you realize so long after the loss that you're still not the same person you used to be; that this chronic soul injury just won't heal up. This is tough medicine to take, but more difficult still is coming to feel quite sure that you'll never be that person again. It's humbling to know you've been internally altered: death has interrupted your plans, severed your relationships, and rewritten the script for you.

And strangely (or perhaps quite understandably) those acute attacks of despair are the very moments when I feel closest to my father, as if the pain somehow allows me to remove the space and time which separate us and I can press my head against his chest and hear his heartbeat once more. These tragic times are somehow oddly comforting even as they kick me in the gut.

And it is *this* odd healing sadness which I'll carry for the remainder of my days; the nexus between total devastation and gradual restoration. It is the way your love outlives your loved one.

I've walked enough of this road to realize that it is my road now. This is not just a momentary detour; it's the permanent state of affairs. I will have many good days and many moments of gratitude and times of welcome respite; I already do—but I'm never fully getting over this loss.

This is the cost of sharing your life with someone worth missing.

Four years into my walk in Grief Valley, I've resigned myself to the truth that this a lifetime sentence. At the end of my time here on the planet, I will either be reunited with my father in some glorious mystery or simply reach my last day of mourning his loss.

Either way, I'm beginning to rest in this simple truth:

The day I'll stop grieving—is the day I stop breathing.

# CHAPTER THIRTY FIVE

# An Open Letter to Those Who Still Give a Damn

It's exhausting to give a damn, isn't it?

To be a person of compassion in a time when compassion is in such great demand?

To wake up every morning on days like these and push back against predatory politicians and toxic systems and human rights atrocities and acts of treason and spiritual leadership failures and Trump Tweet Tantrums. The volume and the relentlessness of the threats can be wearying.

You may have noticed.

I think you have.

And you're not simply carrying around these big picture, larger systemic sicknesses and political realities—but the people behind them: the names and the faces and the lives of specific human beings who are under unprecedented duress right now; people whose stories you listen to and know and are living with; people you dearly love.

And, day after day, all these massive realities and these individual stories begin to accumulate upon your shoulders and in your clenched jaw and in your elevated heart rate and in the knot in your stomach that returns every morning when you check Twitter or turn on the news or step out into your community or just walk into the kitchen. You see so many reasons for grief, so many places compassion is so needed— yet seems so very scarce.

And worst of all is how many people, both distant and very close to you, just don't seem to give a damn; how the pain of other people simply doesn't register in them anymore.

It seems like fewer and fewer people are capable of even an entry-level empathy for the suffering around them, and you're seriously considering joining their ranks because of how tired you are of carrying both your own compassion and their share, too, for a hurting humanity.

Not long after the election, I purchased a blood pressure monitor—not one of those manual base models, either. I went high-end, top of the line: full upper arm cuff, automated pressure, digital readout...the works. I soon stopped using it, though, as it was a daily reminder of how stressed I was. I don't look at it any longer. I don't measure my blood pressure anymore. Now, I just assume it's dangerously high.

All of us who give a damn have new dangers assailing our hearts these days. It is in this time of relentless urgency and sustained trauma and prolonged fatigue and profound fracture that you and I find ourselves.

I'm not sure why you're reading this, but it's probably because you're still a damn-giver; because you are a fierce lover of the planet and humanity—of people who don't look or worship or sound like you. As a result, you probably find yourself pissed off, disconnected, isolated, worn out, and exhausted because so few people are as moved by the need around them as you are.

Whether you're an activist or a minister or a parent or a caregiver or just a citizen of the planet who is moved by other people's suffering—you likely feel the immeasurable heaviness of these days. Sure, speed and activity can mask it for a while, but if you stop long enough, the reality of the fatigue catches up to you and you can measure the toll it's all taken on you.

I want you to measure it; I want you to reckon with how tired you are. I want you to hear yourself exhale with the heavy sigh of someone who feels the weight of it all.

There is a cost to compassion—a personal price tag to cultivate empathy in days when cruelty is trending. In your body and in your head and in your midst, there is a collateral damage to you giving a damn when others do not, and it manifests itself in many ways: irritability, impatience, physical illness, emotional eating, addictive behavior, the inability to be present to the people who love you, an obsession with social media, a fixation on how jacked up everything is.

Notice these things in yourself today, and give them your attention.
Extend yourself some of that compassion you're so willing to extend to the world.
Take some time to step away from the fray and the fight. It will still be there when you return, and you'll be better able to face it.

Friend, I know you're exhausted. If you're not exhausted right now, your empathy is busted.
But I also know that you aren't alone.
Millions of people are as tired as you are right now.
We, too, live in disbelief at how calloused so many people we know and love have become.
We, too, are incredulous while witnessing our elected leaders and parents and neighbors and pastors and favorite aunts abandon any semblance of kindness.
We, too, feel the fatigue of believing we're doing this damn-giving alone.
You are in good company...so keep going.
Fight like hell to keep your heart soft, even while so many people have become hardened.
Yes, the world is upside-down right now, but we can make it right—one beautiful act of decency at a time.
Get some rest and keep going.
The world needs more people like you.

Blessed are the damn-givers, for they will right-side the world.

CHAPTER THIRTY SIX

# Dying to Leave, Trying to Live: My Depression Journey

*Trigger warning: suicide, self-harm*

"I'm done living."

It was a few days after Christmas and I was sitting in a car outside our Central New York hotel, with heavy snow swiftly obscuring the world outside the windows. My tears turned cold as they ran down my cheeks, and my labored breath shot white clouds like fireworks in front of me.

After months of a slow and steady slide into a now lingering sadness—all my exhausted mind could process was, "I'm done."

I didn't want to kill myself—at least I didn't process it that way in that moment; I just felt as though I'd exhausted every possibility that a living person could not to feel like this: prayer, therapy, meditation, medication, working out, nature, journaling, art, breathing exercises, positive thinking—and it was all presently failing me. I'd simply run out of options and energy, and I was done.

It didn't matter that all the objective evidence of my life testified that I should be happy, that I was fortunate, that I had so much to be grateful for, so much to want to live for—none of that registered in those moments; none of that tipped the scales toward hope. The dire story I told myself didn't require data. It never does.

That's what people don't understand about those of us who live with the inner monsters: Intellectually, we understand that this makes no sense, which is often part of the problem. We don't just feel terrible—we feel guilty for feeling so terrible. We have a chronic pain with no discernible source, so we hurt and we feel stupid for hurting. Telling us how much we have to live for and how good our lives are sometimes makes us feel worse.

For many people, life can be a daily battle to stay positive.

For people with severe depression, life can be a daily battle to *stay*.

While everyone finds themselves occasionally slipping into moments of expected sadness when trouble or conflict or tragedy visit—we are often standing hopelessly at the precipice of the abyss for no good reason, staring into the black void and wondering why we're here again: dying to leave and trying to live.

Depression brings a heavy and hovering despair that requires no measurable cause to exist, so when tangible difficulties do come, when actual difficult circumstances and struggles finally arrive—they can become the final straw; they can push us over that edge.

I think that's what people without mental illness don't understand about days like these...when so much cruelty is being cultivated and when leaders are manufacturing such prolific violence and when decency is in such great demand: They are potentially deadly days for us. The outside world *and* our own heads agree that it's hopeless.

I managed to pull myself out that night. I'm not sure how. The hows and whys of who makes it in this battle and who doesn't usually defy understanding. Lots of good, loving, intelligent, faithful people don't make it.

I only know that somehow I stepped back into jagged, bloody trenches of life and decided to keep fighting. I had just enough in my reserves of energy or I grabbed a fleeting moment and got enough clarity then to realize that I needed to keep going; to step out of that car and out of that moment. Then I let a few people into the Hell I was walking through so that I wasn't walking it alone.

But I could easily have not done those things—I could have been one of the millions of people whose exhaustion simply won in the disorienting chaos of the swirling sadness.

And the thing about it is—if I *had* given up, if I *had* walked further into that done-ness to something worse—no one would have seen it coming. I would have simply been another person with so much to live for, being eulogized by stunned loved ones who were trying to make sense of the senseless.

Like so many people who struggle with depression, I can be really good at hiding it. We have to be. It's part of the gig. We hide because we feel like a burden and we hide because we hate admitting that we're losing.

I tell you that because there are likely people around you whom you love dearly...and they're hiding it as well. Do your best to see them and to step into their lives and to let them know they matter and that you want them to stay. Know, too, if they decide they can't stay that you did what you could to help. Sometimes all the love in the world isn't enough to save people. It's really difficult from the outside to speak louder than the voices in someone's head.

I'm still here a year later. I'm usually glad I am.

It has been beautiful and horrible—and it's rarely been easy. Mental illness doesn't afford you much *easy*.

I do want to stay, so I still do all the things I can do to avoid feeling the way I sometimes still feel. I have a daily regimen of prayer, therapy, meditation, medication, working out, nature, journaling, art, breathing exercises, and positive thinking—and yet there are still fleeting moments when I look down and see only the void.

Until some miracle cure comes, the millions of us who walk this nonsensical, exhausting road will be here alongside you doing what we can do: dying to leave and trying to live.

*Note: If you're struggling with depression, desire to self-harm, or suicidal thoughts, talk to someone at the National Suicide Prevention lifeline at 1-800-273-8255.*

*You are worth fighting for.*

# CHAPTER THIRTY SEVEN

# I Just Want to Leave This World

Some days I just want to leave this world.

Living here much longer simply feels like an emotional impossibility these days.

The cruelty is too prevalent, the atrocities too pervasive, the fractures beyond repair.

It is an exercise in diminishing returns each morning as I expend the necessary energy required to protect the fragile embers of hope still remaining within me. With so much threatening to snuff it out, it's difficult to breathe in this "short-on-hope" atmosphere. It's as if my chest can't fully expand and I feel myself slowly suffocating beneath the weight of how not-right it all is and how few people seem to notice.

Every day I do my best to gather my strength, redouble my resolve, and step out into the brokenness and enmity, bleeding heart affixed to my sleeve. But a disorienting spiritual nausea soon grips me as I try to navigate the now wildly-shifting bedrock of what I once believed and the people I thought I knew and the home I imagined I had. No ground feels solid anymore.

To be a deeply feeling person in a time when empathy has become a middle-digit partisan slur doesn't seem sustainable and neither does staying—so today I just want to leave this world.

I want to leave its coldness forever in my rearview, to run into anything else because even the terrifying *what could be* beyond this place seems more inviting right now than the terrible *what is*. Some days I want to step swiftly from here into hereafter, because *here* is too painful to endure.

But that's just the sadness talking.

Leaving isn't really an option because this is still my home, because I am still tethered here to people I love fiercely; because there is still so much unfinished music inside me; because whatever force of life still resides here beating defiantly in the center of my chest isn't fully extinguished yet—and because I refuse to depart until it is.

And so today I just want to leave this world.

I want to leave it *more compassionate than I found it*.

I want people here who are pressed up hard against desperation to encounter rest in me; for them to feel less alone in the grief and the disbelief they carry on their rubbed-raw shoulders and to be able to exhale again.

*I want to leave this world more just than when I arrived.*

At the end of my time, I want to know that while I was here I spent every bit of the unearned currency of my privilege to make room at the table for the excluded and uninvited and unloved; to create spaces of refuge where people experience true belonging in my presence even if few other places offer them respite.

*I want to leave this world lighter than it was when I got here.*

I want to be a source of fits of laughter and kind acts and joyful exchanges that are medicinal to the souls of people afflicted by the heaviness of loss, disappointment, failure, and rejection—to bring lift and light in the face of so much deflation.

Yes, I want to leave this world safer and kinder and funnier and more decent—which means staying as long as I can and filling up my days with as much that affirms life as I can manage, until my last day arrives.

It means speaking words of truth and love even when silence would be the less turbulent path: engaging the cruelty, confronting the atrocities, and placing myself into the fractures so that, hopefully, even in ways I can't see or measure in the moment—some healing might come.

I figure that's the best use of the time and the place and the story I'm standing in right now.

One day I'm going to leave this world for good.

But today I'm going to leave it better.

CHAPTER THIRTY EIGHT

# In the Time Before You Say Goodbye to Those You Love

The last time I spoke to my father was on the telephone.

He was departing on a cruise to celebrate his 70th birthday and we'd unexpectedly caught him a few minutes before he left port. I could hear steel drums in the background as he excitedly talked about the trip ahead. We briefly shared stories of our Halloween shopping experience; the kids had just picked out costumes at the store. Then we wished him a great time and happy birthday, and told him we loved him and would talk to him in a few days.

He went to dinner with my mom and other relatives, explored the ship for a bit—then went to bed and never woke up.

Just like that, our time together here was over. Forty-four years would have to be enough for me. It wasn't.

I often wish I'd have known in those few, seemingly uneventful minutes that this was the last time I'd hear his voice while he was alive. I would have listened more intently, I would have savored every word—I probably wouldn't have hung up.

I'd thought many times before about the day I'd no longer have my father in my life, but I never imagined it would be *that* day, that *this* would end up being that final *I love you*. That's usually how this works. Death rarely gives us the specifics in advance; in fact, our last days and moments and conversations with the people we love often feel so shockingly mundane—until we see them in the rearview mirror. Then, they're breathtaking. Then, they're dramatic pivot points. Then, they're our last goodbyes.

My father's death has changed me in more ways than I can list or even understand, but one of the things it's done is to remind me of the separations coming. I am more and more aware of the way our time with people actually works: We add memories all while losing minutes—addition and subtraction in concert. Many days, I catch myself inventorying the relationships with those I love and realizing that they, too, will all reach this place I reached with my father on that day five years ago: the spot where one of us is gone and the other left behind. I'm trying to make better use of the time before then.

The moment we meet the people we love, the clock starts ticking. The very second our paths cross with another human being, we actually begin counting down. Every meaningful relationship we have in our lives exists in the ever-shrinking time before we say goodbye to them. We should love and move and speak with the urgency befitting this truth.

I wonder how differently we'd treat the ordinary moments with people we love if we realized that they were anything but ordinary, if we could somehow, in those very seconds, sense that we are rapidly losing daylight—not to depress or frighten us, but to wake us up.

I had forty-four years with my father and it wasn't nearly enough. I didn't want that to be the last conversation we had, but it was. Sixteen thousand and sixty days: that was the amount of time between our hello and goodbye.

I don't know how much time I'll have with my mother, with my wife, my kids, my friends—but I know it won't be enough. I'm trying to remember that when I take them for granted, when I waste moments, when I postpone saying things, when I feel like we'll have forever.

Time is running out with the people who make your heart feel at home––with those who give this life meaning; with the ones you sleep next to; with the ones who'll call you on Father's Day; the ones you argue with as you walk out the door; and the ones you're not speaking to anymore. Your last exchange may be while hurriedly escorting them to the bus stop or in an abbreviated midday text or in a screaming match followed by estrangement. It may be in a quick phone call with steel drums in the distance.

Say the words you feel like you'll have more time to say later; you may not.
Be honest and be clear.

Give kind words and speak truth and offer forgiveness.
And when you're talking to those whose presence you treasure and whose absence you'll grieve deeply, listen intently and savor every word as if it's the last conversation you'll have.

It could be—and you probably won't know.

Do all that you can to make good use of this beautiful, fragile, glorious extraordinary time with the people you love...the time before you say goodbye.

CHAPTER THIRTY NINE

# Acknowledging Our Grief Anniversaries

I always struggle on sunny Saturday mornings.

It was a brilliantly blue-skyed September Saturday four years ago when I bounded down the stairs on the way to the gym and noticed my phone vibrating on the hallway table. The caller ID told me that it was Eric, my youngest brother, so I rushed to answer; I was eager to catch up. Had I known what he was going to tell me ten seconds later, I wouldn't have answered.

That was the moment I found out my father was gone.

As only those who mourn the loss of someone they love deeply understand, sunny Saturday mornings have never been the same for me. They are now a Grief Anniversary—a perpetual, involuntary holiday where my heart marks its injury over and over and over again without me getting a say in the matter. Since that terrible day, regardless of what I've been in the middle of, there has rarely been a Saturday morning when I have not found myself reliving that moment in some way, my mind jarred from its routine to momentarily eulogize my father once again.

I wish it was the only such occasion, as I could probably handle feeling this horrible once a week—but that's not how this works.

Most people think that grieving is about the big annual events—about Christmases and birthdays and the like, and of course it is. But the brutal truth—one that only those who continue to live after someone dear to them is gone can rightly fathom—is that these other quiet anniversaries are equally devastating and far more frequent.

In the wake of losing a loved one, everything in your life becomes a potential surprise memorial. Out of nowhere, you are broadsided by days of the week or times of day or numbers on the calendar or songs that were playing or cologne you were wearing or the feel of the grass beneath your knees as you fell at the news. These seemingly incessant reminders force you once again to observe the loss anew.

And since these days and times and triggers aren't obvious to most people in our lives—and since we don't have the time or the words to describe them all—they are usually unaware of just how much and just how often we mourn. Even those who are closest to us and care for us greatly remain largely oblivious to our recurring sadness. Our grief can feel like a very lonely journey, which it is in many ways because it is specific to us and to the one we've lost. It is a customized but hidden wound.

I've tried to remember this because it helps me realize that most people I encounter every day are doing this continual memorializing of someone they love, too. Like me, they have these constant pinpricks to the heart they are experiencing at any given moment. Like me, they could be internally reeling for what seems to be no apparent reason. This very ordinary day for me could be a day of extraordinary mourning for them.

When someone you love deeply dies, the calendar of your life is altered forever. It gets divided into the time before and the time after that moment. I'll probably never have another uninterrupted sunny Saturday morning again. My mind will likely always find a way of marking the occasion and reminding me once more that normal is a very relative term now. In this way, each moment is another chance to grieve my father, another potential opportunity to measure the depth of my love for him by the level of my loss in his absence.

Today, for a million reasons, you might very well find yourself observing the absence of someone you miss dearly and, though it will be a rather uneventful day to the world around you, it will be a National Day of Mourning in the center of your own aching heart.

Please know that you are not alone, dear friend. I acknowledge the pain within you and I observe this day along with you.

Peace, on this Grief Anniversary.

Be encouraged.

# CHAPTER FORTY

# I'm Really Tired Of Hatred

Yesterday while picking up lunch, I ran into a friend I hadn't seen in a few months.

After exchanging surprised greetings and a fierce hug, she stopped abruptly, looked genuinely concerned—and said, "Are you OK? You look tired today."

After weathering the initial sting of her honest but uninvited commentary, I assured her she was somewhat incorrect in her evaluation.

"Not just today." I remarked matter of factly. "This is how I look now—I'm always tired."

She smiled widely and then leaned in with genuine concern and quietly pressed for details: "So what are you tired of?"

I couldn't come up with an answer that seemed sufficient in the thirty seconds we had remaining before our takeout orders were ready (and honestly, I didn't feel right baring my soul surrounded by complete strangers in front of a full deli case) so I laughed and said, "Oh, you know!"—and quickly changed the subject.

But on the way home, her question was still hanging there in my head: What *am* I tired of?

Hatred.

That's it. I'm tired of hatred—like, *really* tired.

I'm tired of waking every morning and seeing that we're in another unnecessary and preventable constitutional crisis.

I'm tired of having to once again channel the adrenaline to confront a new onslaught of real and manufactured emergencies.

I'm tired of having to desperately appeal to public servants to do the decent and humane thing and see them again flatly refuse.

I'm tired of trying to convince professed followers of Jesus that they're supposed to care about other people.

I'm tired of dancing through minefields at family gatherings; doing verbal gymnastics to sidestep relational explosions; and to keep loving people I've recently learned unsettling things about.

I'm tired of scrolling through racist, anti-LGBTQ, anti-immigrant, anti-Semitic hate speech filling my social media mentions.

I'm tired of being reminded daily of the white supremacy that my former church friends are so terribly afflicted with.

I'm tired of seeing stories of newly-emboldened bigots showing up as neighbors, elementary school teachers, local politicians, and coffee shop patrons—because they feel a kindred embittered spirit in the White House.

I'm tired of boastful, nonsensical, intentionally-provocative presidential tweets littered with Democratic slander, wall-building taunts, and abject lies.

I am so damn tired of hatred—and yes, I'm tired of hating it all too.

I'm tired of continually confronting ugliness—and of the increasing ugliness it brings out in me as I do.

I'm tired of walking into a room and trying to calculate inside my head how many of them there are—and resenting human beings I've never met based on my evaluation.

I'm tired of assuming the worst in people because of the bumper sticker on their car or the red hat atop their head or the channel they get their news from.

I'm tired of the impatience and irritability always sitting just below the surface of my countenance, and how often it breaks violently through and into my day in angry words in traffic or expletives spoken under my breath or easy frustration with the normal inconveniences of life.

I'm tired of regularly losing my religion as I fight both for and with my faith tradition: being anything but Christlike while advocating for the teachings of Jesus.

I'm tired of feeling a growing hopelessness when I see the people we're becoming.

I know this fight is emotionally and physically exhausting, that there is a profound personal cost for hating things, even things that merit hatred. I know that it makes my heart less buoyant and far more susceptible to sinking into despair.

I'm trying to make sure I stay a loving person opposing things that make me angry and not a perpetually angry person— but it's difficult to tell when you're swimming in so much enmity every day.

I want to leave a legacy of kindness, a compassionate wake in the waters of this world so that other people who are similarly fatigued by the hatred they encounter here find rest in me.

Maybe that's all any of us can do: perpetuate decency and goodness and generosity in the infinitesimal space of the next choice in front of us.

Maybe, if we make this world a little bit more loving in the small and the close and the present, maybe...just maybe the ripples will eventually reach the big and the distant and the future.

Then maybe everyone who's as fully tired of hatred as we are will finally get some rest.

# CHAPTER FORTY ONE

# Please Stop Calling Suicide Victims Selfish or Weak

Soon after news broke about the death of Linkin Park singer Chester Bennington, amid the flood of condolences and the raw expressions of grief and shock, came the others...the ones who are never far, always hiding just out of view, ever ready to crawl out from the cracks.

In moments like these, they surface to offer flippant, callous, armchair sermons about how selfish suicide is; about how cowardly the dead person was; about why he or she should have thought of their children, spouses, loved ones.
They add insult to fatal injury by heaping shame upon a suffering

that had already proven to be too much for someone to bear. These people somehow feel fine critiquing dead strangers before they've even been buried.

I've come to realize that there is only one kind of person who says things like this about those who take their own lives: a person who has never been where Chester Bennington was in his final moments, or where Chris Cornell was, or where 121 people in the US are every single day—where many are in the seconds it takes for you to read these words. The people who say such things are those who've never been pushed to the precipice of their very will to live—because of mental illness or acute trauma or severe addiction. These people have the luxury of ignorance, fortunately for them; they've never walked through this unrivaled internal Hell and wanted nothing more than to get out.

When you are in that desperate, frantic, lightless moment of despair—reason fails. There is no processing of things that seem so clear to people sitting calmly in parks and at desks and in living rooms where they offer detached, knee-jerk commentary— while in their right minds, unclouded, lucid, and sober.

That is what mental illness does; that is what addiction does; that is what depression does: Working against you alone or together, they convince your head that nothing matters. This terrible moment will not pass, nothing will get better, and you are fully, irreparably, and permanently f*cked. It doesn't have to make sense; it doesn't require objective proof; and it has no need for logic—you just feel it. In those moments, the only thing you want is escape—and the choices people make in those moments are beyond what any of us have the right to criticize from the outside.

I've never battled substance abuse or addiction but, for a couple of decades, I have carried depression that has been terrifyingly heavy at times. And despite prayer and counseling and meditation and medication, there have been moments when the sadness became so overwhelming that nothing helped; not my career or my family or all the objective data I had that everything was good and that I should just feel better. I wouldn't have said I was suicidal then—I just didn't want to live. What got me through and what gets some people through when others fall is one of the greatest mysteries of this life. Some people make it and some people don't—and the former aren't any wiser or stronger or better. They're just very, very fortunate.

Suicide isn't cowardly.
It's not weakness.
It isn't selfish.
It's born of a hopelessness that can imagine no other way out.
It is a thick, pitch black haze created by powerful personal demons that prevent you from seeing light.

People like to say that suicide is a permanent solution to a temporary problem, and they're right—but those standing in the darkest places can't see that from where they are.

When someone takes their own life, we can view it as a tragedy for their loved ones; as a reason to mourn their leaving; as a squandering of what that life may have one day become; we can even be really angry at the senselessness of the loss.

But we should never use the moment to insult the dead by trying to shame them after they're gone. Believe me, they really wanted to stay.

They did the very best they could in the worst seconds of their lives. They were as brave and strong and selfless as they were able to be in those moments.

There but for the grace of God go the critics.

May you always be such strangers to the dark.

Friend, if you're struggling with depression, addiction, desire to self-harm, or suicidal thoughts, talk to someone. Help can be found at suicidepreventionlifeline.org and twloha.com and befrienders.org and thetrevorproject.org now. You are worth fighting for.

# CHAPTER FORTY TWO

# Things I've Learned Since My Father Died

This is my least favorite day of the year.

Today, September 13, is my father's birthday. Five years ago he turned 70, and that night he passed away in his sleep while on a cruise with my mom and brother.

An atomic bomb detonated in my life as I learned that news, and I'm honestly still trying to climb out from the rubble left behind. As people who grieve understand, you don't ever really get past it. You may have days or seasons where you believe you've reached a clearing—some sort of emotional distance from it all. You begin to function at a very high level for long periods of time, and occasionally you even begin to think you're "healed." Then suddenly, something surfaces: a scent, a thought, a song, a milestone, or a day on the calendar—and, in an instant, it's Ground Zero and Day 1 all over again, and you're buried and broken and you can't see the light.

This is where I am today. I am beginning again: fresh wounds, new grief, history repeating. I'm not ashamed about this. I'm okay not being okay.

People say that when you lose someone you love, you learn things that you couldn't learn any other way. This is true.

I've learned a deeper compassion for people in pain.
I've learned the near superhuman strength of my mother.
I've learned how once ordinary objects become sacred relics.
I've learned how much you can hurt and still hold it together on the surface.
I've learned that the acute pain gives you closer proximity to the people you've lost.
I've learned that old memories returning are like surprise packages from Heaven.
I've learned that death will challenge your faith in ways you never imagined.
I've learned that after three years, you still reach for the phone to call them.
I've learned that the way you grieve is the right way to grieve, because it is your way.
I've learned that you'd gladly trade everything you own for thirty more seconds with them.
I've learned how to cry in a restaurant bathroom and come out as if nothing happened.
I've learned to accept that my daughter will never remember her Papa, and to be okay hating this.

I've learned the joy in recognizing your loved ones in your laugh, your reflection, your hands, your children.

I've learned to resent strangers who have their fathers and grandfathers and no empty chairs during the holidays.

I've learned that on some days, though not suicidal, you'll wish you could die just to see them again.

I've learned that even though good people try to help, ultimately you have to grieve alone.

I've learned that no matter how old you are, you never stop needing your Daddy.

I've learned the horrible accuracy of all those clichés about how we never have enough time with the people we love; about how there are no ordinary days; and about the tissue paper-thin fragility of life.

I've learned that tears are a tribute.

I've learned that death just sucks, and that any other spin on it is just a valiant but failing effort to make lemonade out of some really bitter fruit.

But, mostly, I've learned just how big a hole someone can leave in your life; how massive a gap there is when they're gone, and how we all fill that space for someone.

I do much of my work in words written for other people, trying to speak about life with some kind of clarity, so that they can find themselves in those words and be encouraged. I'm not sure these words will do that, but these words are for me because I need to say them—as prayers, as medicine, as thank yous.

Today is my father's birthday. He taught me so much in life. He is still teaching me.

Happy Birthday, Dad.

# CHAPTER FORTY THREE

# Don't Forget to Be Happy

Welcome to another day.

You probably didn't give much thought to the fact that you're here, that you woke up.

You likely haven't stopped to breathe in deeply and slowly, to feel the air expand your chest and then let it fall slowly as the air departs on your instruction.

You probably haven't taken a second to realize that you're alive.

There's a good chance your mind has already been overtaken by all the things you need to do, the tasks at hand, the appointments you have, everything filling up the small white block of your calendar assigned to today, all the worries that made sleep difficult last night, the noisy parade of bad news you're already scrolling through.

You're already running so fast, so quickly.

Because of all the urgent and terrible and necessary demands pulling at you from every direction, I bet you went from lying down into a full sprint in a matter of seconds...not giving your body and mind a chance to ease into it all, to be intentional about this moment, to decide not what you'll do today—but how you'll *be* today.

You're likely going to be really busy, and since you are—I don't want you to forget something important:

I don't want you to forget to be happy.

I don't want you to fritter away the next 86,400 seconds as they skyrocket by you from the present and into the past, never filling them with the things that give you joy or generate gratitude or register contentment.

Today it's going to be difficult for you to remember that *this* is life: that you are not waiting on a day that is coming in which to do all that you dream of doing; or to say everything you should say to people you love; or to create and build and write and make the beautiful things stored up inside you.

If not reminded, you likely won't remember that this is not a day to RSVP for some future living you'll do somewhere off on the horizon.

You and the sunlight are both here now.

I'd hate to see you procrastinate away living for another time—when *this* is the living time.

Because it was not a guarantee that you'd wake up today.

Many people didn't.

They didn't get to feel the rise and fall of their chests.

They didn't get to stop and notice they are alive.

They are missing this day that you and I are present for.

If they *had* opened their eyes today and joined us here, they'd likely already be running, too. They'd likely already be at the precipice of making the same mistake you and I can make if we're not careful.

They, too, might be seduced by the calendar and distracted by their obligations and weighed down by the tragedies—so much that they would forget to fully live in this small twenty-four hour sliver of time and space in front of them.

I realize that conditions aren't perfect today for any of this, but trust me—they will not be tomorrow, either.

There will again be things you need to do, tasks at hand, appointments you've made, everything filling up the small white block of your calendar assigned to that day, all the worries that will have made sleeping tonight difficult, and the noisy parade of bad news you'll be scrolling through should you reach the morning.

All the more reason—on this imperfect day—you need to do something that declares you will not be so overwhelmed by all that is not right, that you refrain from living well.

Fill your time with the people and animals who make you feel loved, with moments spent in the places that refresh and inspire you: with creating and making and dreaming the glorious stuff that cannot wait because they can only be born by you today.

Please put joy on your agenda today.

Don't make it wait.

Create space for it.

Work for justice and be outraged when it is denied.

Passionately oppose every bit of inhumanity that you can.

Never grow comfortable with cruelty or brutality.

But, amidst the countless appointment reminders, calendar notifications, and sticky note prompts that keep you focused on all that seemingly needs to be done—include one more critical reminder, even if you have to tattoo it on your heart:

*Welcome to another day. Don't forget to be happy.*

# CHAPTER FORTY FOUR

# Grieving People Need You Most After the Funeral

My father died suddenly while on vacation three years ago. The event rattled the bedrock of my life in ways that are difficult to describe, teaching me lessons I couldn't have learned any other way.

One of the truths I discovered is that when you lose someone you love...people show up.

Almost immediately, they surround you with social media condolences and texts and visits and meals and flowers. They come with good hearts, with genuine compassion, and they truly want to support you in those moments. The problem is that you're neither prepared nor particularly helped by the outpouring of support so soon.

The early days of grief are a hazy, dizzying, moment by moment response to a trauma that your mind simply can't wrap itself around. You are what I like to call a *Grief Zombie*—outwardly moving but barely there. You aren't really functioning normally by any reasonable measurement, so that huge crush of people feels like thousands of cars have suddenly been diverted onto a one-lane back road—the unexpected traffic overwhelms the system. You can't absorb it all. Often, it actually hurts.

This usually happens until the day of the funeral, when the flood of support begins to subside almost immediately. Over the coming days, the calls and visits gradually become less frequent as people begin to return to normal with lives already in progress...right about the time the bottom drops out for you.

Just as the shock begins to wear off and the haze is lifted and you start to feel the full gravity of the loss, just as you get a clear look at the massive crater in your heart...you find yourself alone.

People don't leave you because they're calloused or unconcerned—they're just unaware. Most people understand grief as an *event*, not as the permanent alteration to life that it is. So they stay connected with you until the funeral; they imagine that when the service ends, somehow you, too, can move ahead—that there is some *end point* to your mourning.

But the thing you learn as you grieve is that grief has no shelf life; you will feel this loss as long as you breathe—long after the memorial service and even longer after most people are prepared to stay. Again, they still love you dearly; they just have their own roads to walk.

Sometimes people leave because they suddenly feel estranged by the death. They may have been used to knowing you as part of a couple or as a family, and they aren't able to navigate the new dynamic the loss has created. They simply don't know how to relate to you the way they once did...and so they withdraw.

Or sometimes people see you from a distance and mistake your visible stability for the absence of need, as if the fact that you're functioning in public doesn't mean you don't fall apart all the time when you're alone—you do. We all carry the grief as bravely and competently as we can in public, but none of us is strong enough to shoulder it alone. People often say of a grieving person, "They're so strong," but they're not. They're doing what they have to in order to survive. They need you to come alongside them.

Other times, people avoid you because they worry that they will say the wrong thing; they fear that somehow they will remind you of your loved one and cause you unnecessary pain. Trust me, the grieving don't lack for reminders; they are intimately aware of the absence in their lives. Your acknowledgement of their loss actually makes them feel better. It gives them consent to live with their grief, and to know that they can be both wounded and normal.

Friends, what I'm saying is that it's wonderful to be present for people when tragedy occurs. It's a beautiful thing to express your love and support for those you love in any way you feel is right in those first few days. It does matter. No compassion is ever wasted.

But if there's anything I would tell you as someone who's walked through the Grief Valley, it's that the time your presence is most needed and most powerful is during those days and weeks and months and years after the funeral—when most people have withdrawn and the road is most isolating. It is in the countless ordinary moments that follow when grief sucker punches you and, again, you feel it all fully.

It's been five years since I lost my father and, on many days, the pain is as present and profound as it was that very first day.

So friend, remind yourself to reach out to people long after the services and memorials have concluded, because...

Death is a date on the calendar, but grief *is* the calendar.

# CHAPTER FORTY FIVE

# With the Time You Have Left Here

"We should do a CAT scan just to rule out some things." the urgent care doctor said.

Before I could ask him, he responded to the question that had immediately formed inside my throbbing head.

"—things like aneurysms or tumors."

A few minutes later, I was sitting on a sheet of onion-skin examining table paper, beneath the raking fluorescent light of an antiseptic, nondescript hospital room—and imagining the worst. My mind rocketed to the dire news he could have for me in a few minutes; just what he might say when he returned; and the terrifying dominoes that would fall afterward. I imagined telling my wife and considering treatment options and explaining it to our kids and paying bills and changing vacation plans—and a hundred different things that, while I was sitting there, seemed like a pending reality.

It's one of those moments when you remember that you're not permanent; that you aren't superhuman; that this will all be over someday—and far sooner than we realize or want.

The examining room door flew open and abruptly interrupted my dizzying daymare, already well in progress.

"Everything came back negative," the doctor said, "so we're in good shape."

He kept talking, but I didn't hear much after that. I was too busy trying to fight back tears.

And just like that, the tidal wave of terror subsided, the color returned to my cheeks, and I exhaled deeper than I had in recent memory. A few minutes later, I was outside watching the sun peeking over the tree line and feeling the breeze against my face and being relieved.

*So—I'm not dying,* I thought to myself and then replied,—*well, not yet anyway.*

Since that morning, I've been thinking about the fact that I didn't get an exemption with that good news—just a temporary reprieve. One day, the news won't be good. One day, I won't get to exhale. One day, I might not see the sun.

Some people think it's morbid to consider their demise, but I think it's helpful. We should remember that we all have an expiration date; that our days here are finite; that we all have far less time than we want. We should give ourselves the gift of doing the math of our remaining existence.

If you're reading this, chances are you have—at best—six or so decades left here (but likely far less than that). There is a number that exists and, while you can't see it, that number represents the sunrises you have remaining.

And the question I asked myself as I left the hospital is the same one I'll ask you:

*What do you want to do with the time you have left here?*

How many of those precious, fleeting, irretrievable-once-they're-gone seconds do you want to spend:

postponing a dream you've been carrying around?
holding a grudge against someone you can't seem to forgive?
obsessing about your waistline or hairline or worry lines?
waiting for someone else's consent to be happy?
being a bystander to injustice?
looking for approval from strangers on social media?
being less than the most authentic version of yourself?
compromising your convictions to keep the peace?
staying in a relationship where the other person doesn't give what you give?
beating yourself up for the stupid stuff your younger self did?

It isn't easy to get out of the well-worn ruts our minds make for us. The ordinary days have a way of lulling us into believing there isn't any urgency to them; that somewhere off in the distance, we'll actually begin doing the important stuff we need to do. We'll start living someday.

This is just a reminder that *today* is the day to do that important stuff. Today is someday.

This is a reminder that your days *are* numbered, and since you don't know *what* that number is—you should live the hell out of this day.

Ask anything.
Say everything.
Give yourself a break.
Show mercy.
Have the cake.
Notice how fast your kids are growing.
Treasure the lines on your face as mementos of grief and joy.
Tell someone you love them while they can still hear you.
Stop being your own Kryptonite.
Find a hill worth dying on and take it.
Have a second piece of cake.

This day, as ordinary and uneventful as it seems—is one of the relatively few you have left.

Do something worthy of it.

When Death shows up to give you news you didn't want and didn't see coming, may it interrupt you in the act of really living.

# CHAPTER FORTY SIX

# On the Day I Die

On the day I die, a lot will happen.

A lot will change.

The world will be busy.

On the day I die, all the important appointments I made will be broken.

The many plans I had yet to complete will remain forever undone.

The calendar that ruled so many of my days will be irrelevant.

All the material things I so chased and guarded and treasured will be left in the hands of others to care for or discard.

The words of my critics which so burdened me will cease to sting or capture me anymore. They will be unable to touch me.

The arguments I believed I'd won here will not serve me or bring me any satisfaction or solace.

All my noisy incoming notifications and texts and calls will go unanswered. Their great urgency will be silenced.

My many nagging regrets will be resigned to the past—where they should have always been.

Every superficial worry about my body that ever caused me labor—my waistline or hairline or frown lines—will fade away.

My carefully crafted image—the one I worked so hard to shape for others—will be left for them to mold as they wish.

The sterling reputation I once struggled so greatly to maintain will be of no concern to me anymore.

All the small and large anxieties that stole sleep from me each night will be rendered powerless.

The deep and towering mysteries about life and death that so consumed my mind will finally be clarified in a way they never could be while I lived.

These things will certainly all be true on the day I die.

Yet, as much as will happen, one more thing will happen on the day I die.

On the day I die, the few people who really know and truly love me will grieve deeply.

They will feel a void.

They will feel cheated.

They will not feel ready.

They will feel as though a part of them has died as well.

And on that day, more than anything in the world, they will want more time with me.

I know this from those I've loved, lost, and still grieve over.

And so, knowing this, while I am still alive I'll try to remember that my time with them is finite and fleeting and so very precious—and I'll do my best not to waste a second of it.

I'll try not to squander a priceless moment worrying about all the other things that will happen on the day I die, because many of those things are either not my concern or beyond my control.

Friends, those other things have an insidious way of keeping you from living even as you live...vying for your attention, competing for your affections.

They rob you of the joy of this unrepeatable, uncontainable, ever-evaporating *Now* with those who love you and want only to share that joy with you.

Don't miss the chance to dance with them while you can.

It's easy to waste so much daylight in the time before you die.

Don't let your life be stolen every day by all that you've been led to believe matters, because on the day you die—the fact is that much of it simply won't.

Yes, you and I will die one day.

But before that day comes, *let us live*.

CPSIA information can be obtained
at www.ICGtesting.com
Printed in the USA
FSHW022333040521
81134FS